D0019209

THE
BEST WORK
of Your
LIFE

Most Perigee Books are available at special quantity discounts for bulk purchases for sales promotions, premiums, fund-raising or educational use. Special books, or book excerpts, can also be created to fit specific needs.

For details, write: Special Markets, The Berkley Publishing Group, 200 Madison Avenue, New York, New York 10016.

THE BEST WORK
of Your
LIFE

PATRICIA V. ALEA

PATRICIA A. MULLINS

A PERIGEE BOOK

A Perigee Book
Published by The Berkley Publishing Group
A member of Penguin Putnam Inc.
200 Madison Avenue
New York, NY 10016

Copyright © 1998 by Patricia Alea and and Patricia Mullins
Book design by Lisa Stokes
Cover design by Charles Björklund

All rights reserved. This book, or parts thereof, may not be reproduced in any form without permission.

First edition: September 1998

Published simultaneously in Canada.

The Penguin Putnam Inc. World Wide Web site address is
http://www.penguinputnam.com

Library of Congress Cataloging-in-Publication Data

Alea, Pat.
    The best work of your life / Pat Alea, Patty Mullins. — 1st ed.
        p.   cm.
    ISBN 0-399-52434-7 (tp)
    1. Vocational guidance.   2. Job hunting.   I. Mullins, Patricia Ann,
1946—   . II. Title.
HF5381. A575   1998
650. 14—dc21

                                                                98-2889
                                                                CIP

Printed in the United States of America

10 9 8 7 6 5 4 3 2 1

This book is dedicated to our late fathers:

Paul A. Mullins

Edward J. Nastali

contents

Preface and Acknowledgments   ix

1   Introduction: The Best Work of Your Life   1

PART ONE · CLARITY

2   From Current Reality to Career Vision   11

3   Your Personal History: Reclaiming Natural Assets   29

4   Work History: Your Skills, Preferences, and Strengths   45

5   Using What You Know to Take Control of Your Career   61

PART TWO · STRATEGY

6   The Ah-ha Résumé   81

7   What's What Networking   106

8   Mapping and Tracking Opportunity   121

9   Initiating Appropriate Strategies   142

10 Professional Identity and Integrity   167

PART THREE · ACTION

11 Printed Material   183

12 Electronic Information   191

13 Networks   201

14 Career Services   209

15 Events   217

Epilogue to Part Three   223

Summary   227

Index   229

preface and acknowledgments

We began writing this book four years ago, almost as soon as we met and started working together. We recognized that our two perspectives created a uniquely extensive and helpful approach to those seeking advice about career and life planning.

Pat's twenty years of working with businesses, government, and associations to achieve organizational goals focused on investing in the individual success of employees.

Patty brought twenty years of experience in research, teaching, and consulting about workplace and workforce issues. She provided important knowledge about the psychology of work and industrial relations issues.

Together we have attempted to combine solid theory with our readers' need to "just do it"—to take action without losing meaningful perspective.

Writing this book was fun and instructive. Daily, our clients would call for consultation and advice, and each time they did we were able to identify the exact chapter and page that we knew would help them once the book was in print. We are confident that your questions about understanding and planning your life and career, whatever they are, will be answered in these pages.

We have several recommendations for readers who want to write a book: go away to nice hotels at midweek for "writing retreats," great resorts in the off-season. Start your book this minute, write it as fast as you can, and spend a few years on revisions. If you are collaborating, pay attention to both the project and the friendship for a doubly rewarding experience. Assemble your hallelujah chorus. Dump your Greek chorus. You'll need lots of backup and you'll have to stay joyful. (This is important advice for career planning as well.)

We have many people to thank, together and individually. For help and support in direct relation to this project, thanks to John Woods and Bob Magnin at CWL Publishing and to Tess Bresnan and John Duff at Perigee/Putnam. Our gratitude regularly goes to Jean Feraca at Wisconsin Public Radio for delivering her listeners to us to call our own. Thanks, too, to Kathi Risley, our producer at WISC-TV. And our enormous gratitude goes to all who have attended our Focus Workshops. We are humbled by what we are able to learn from those who seek our advice.

Pat Alea: I would like to thank my mother, Mary Nastali, who recently "semiretired" and who has worked all her life with meaning and balance. My daughters, Elliott and Amanda Veith, have provided not only real-life stories for this book but their continuing enthusiasm within their own lives as fuel for my work. I extend warmest regards to my e-mail pal Ron Harris, for frequent advice and a constant and refined sensibility about life. And thanks to Bruce Collick, my generous spouse, whose own best work is always to make those around him feel as smart as he is.

Patty Mullins: I would like to thank my mother, Dorothy Mullins, for her good humor and support. She cares very deeply about careers, especially those of the Green Bay Packers. My daughter, Emily Gilbert, astonishes me, as she always has, by doing her best work in every endeavor. She has also taught me that providing career advice to daughters is best done by referral. And, finally, enduring gratitude to my friend Leigh Leslie, who, at a critical moment in my life, opened up the vision that has moved me toward my best work.

Patricia V. Alea
Patricia A. Mullins
Madison, Wisconsin

THE
BEST WORK
of Your
LIFE

introduction:

The Best Work of Your Life

The time is now. The direction is forward. The subject is you. This book is for everyone, from those searching for their first job to workplace veterans. It is for those who are stuck in the rich muck of too many goals, too many dreams, skills, and possibilities. But it is also for those who are prone to act too fast without mucking around enough exploring their potential and preferences.

Following a simple series of jobs can be deadening. Living in fear of downsizing can quite literally make us sick. Being underemployed can sour our view of the world and our value in it. Trying to change our shape or style to grasp any opportunity available can make us lose the personal identity that is the strongest source of our value, to ourselves and to others.

Imagine, instead, operating from a position of power and confidence by understanding the best you have to offer and knowing how to offer it to the world with enthusiasm. That's where the Clarity, Strategy, and Action you'll learn about in this book will take you. That's what it means to be doing the best work of your life, the work that supports what is meaningful to you. But to do "the best work of your life" you first need to get clear about a few things. Then you need to create a strategy for change. Finally, you need to put that strategy into action. In that order.

▪ CLARITY . . . STRATEGY . . . ACTION:
THE THREE KEYS TO YOUR BEST WORK ▪

Clarity =   understanding what you offer and what you need at each stage of your life

Strategy = communicating your value to those who want or need what you offer

Action =   moving steadily forward to get what you need

The art of Clarity, Strategy, and Action, once you master it, will become the steady engine that drives your career. It's never too early or too late to take such control. We have a saying: "There's no such thing as ten years from now." We say it often, anytime we're tempted to think slow or small. We also often say, "If *you* don't manage your career, nobody will. Or worse still, somebody will, but they'll do it their way."

When we are doing less than our best work, we are most likely not in control of our careers and our lives. Gaining the knowledge, skills, and resources necessary to take and maintain control of your life and career is, in itself, hard work. But the alternative is even harder, as you probably already realize.

This book is about understanding all that you have to offer the world and knowing how to offer it with enthusiasm and confidence. We will take you step by step through the phases of Clarity, Strategy, and Action, so that you can enjoy the power and confidence of doing *the best work of your life*.

▪ YOUR WORK AND YOUR LIFE ▪

As you read each section of this book, you'll begin to understand that managing your work within the context of your life allows you not only to do your best work but to plan and be ready for continuous career growth. Our best work serves the changing purposes of our lives.

Without the skills to continuously shape our careers, we can feel dangerously unbalanced. A job that was center stage last week slides into the shadows as family issues compete for our attention. Your career waits in the wings for a cue while you're busy starring in and directing an unfolding drama in your personal life. Health needs, financial crises, spiritual quests, community issues, personal tragedies, or unexpected triumphs—these are life events as real and as important as the work we do, and they can and should shape the way we work.

The best work of your life will be the work that supports what is meaningful to you. The work you do may in part define your sense of purpose, but it is likely to be your best work when it also strengthens and integrates the values and goals that create not just a career but a life. Managing your work will help you manage your life. A warning: learning how to do so is not easy. But we promise you that the results will be well worth your efforts.

We work with individuals and organizations on issues related to life and career planning. Combining personal assessment with high-impact strategies, we base our advice on a "know thyself, know the real world" perspective. Patty's twenty-year background in research and teaching and Pat's twenty years in frontline applications make us an effective team to help individuals identify their priorities and create goals that bring out their best skills.

▪ PERSONAL DIFFERENCES, PERSONAL DIFFICULTIES ▪

As we stated above, this book will guide you through the three keys to the best work of your life: Clarity, Strategy, and Action. Throughout the book we'll often remind you to trust yourself and apply what we offer according to your own needs. To be frank, however, it will be easier for some people than for others, because of personal differences. Gender, age, experience, culture—all these factors influence who we are and how we think, feel, and act. That's normal, but we should keep our differences in mind and try to overcome whatever barriers they may raise in our path to finding the best work of our lives.

For example, some people have difficulty focusing on the personal analysis necessary to achieve genuine clarity. We know this from our experience with clients. This is often a gender issue, as men have been conditioned to downplay personal exploration of their feelings. It may also be a matter of cultural background, a factor of our age and experience, or just the way we were raised.

So when we encourage you, for example, to try to remember the stories most often repeated about you as a baby or small child, we urge you to make the effort to do so. Pay attention to your resistance to self-analysis. Both of us, in developing and applying career management theories in our business, have found that an impulsive resistance often masks the discomfort clients feel in having to face facts. But those facts are about *you*, so it's vital that you learn to face and explore them if you want to achieve the best work of your life.

We have also noticed that some of our clients have been reluctant to create and act on a strategy. They find it very enriching to reflect on their past, sort through the origin of their values, explore every career possibility imaginable—anything but strategically articulate and promote their value in the real world. Again, this is often a gender issue, as many women have been socially conditioned not to take charge. But it can also be a question of culture, of age and experience, or of upbringing.

So when we suggest setting and taking a course of action, we urge you to try to overcome your reluctance to create a strategy and act on it. Pay particular attention to making your action plans concrete, establishing timelines, and determining measurable outcomes. Knowing yourself is very important, but you must act upon what you know if you expect to do the best work of your life.

No matter who you are, no matter what stage you're at in your work life, this book is for you. We know this because we've helped all sorts of people with diverse needs and wishes in every conceivable type of situation. **Don't wait to react to a job or career crisis—take charge now!** If you want to build your future with a clear perspective, so you can be enthusiastic and ready to do the best work of your life, continue reading.

▪ THIS BOOK'S STRUCTURE ▪

Each of the three main sections—Clarity (Chapters 2–5), Strategy (Chapters 6–10), and Action (Chapters 11-15)—offers singular and specific value. Read through the brief outline on the next page so you'll have a good idea of where we'll take you in this book. Some of you will benefit more from a section or a particular chapter than others will. Some chapters will be more difficult for some people. That's natural; we're all different. But we hope you will find in each chapter information that is accessible and valuable. Every concept and every story in this book is meant to enrich and encourage your effort toward doing the best work of your life.

Part One. Clarity: It's About Time

Each chapter in the first section (Chapters 2–5) will focus on a way to gain greater clarity about your life.

Chapter 2. From Current Reality to Career Vision. Most of us have a blurred sense of our busy lives. If we have a vision at all, it's usually too vague to help guide us. In Chapter 2 we urge you to analyze your current situation in an honest and insightful way so you can see more clearly what is actually possible. The progress from your current reality toward new career vision can be achieved in a series of finite steps once you know where you really stand.

Chapter 3. Your Personal History: Reclaiming Natural Assets. Paying attention to who you are will make you a more valuable and powerful person. Why? Because working at odds with your nature creates discomfort, struggle, and a sense of unreality. Chapter 3 will take a look at the earliest indications of your talents and interests to uncover patterns of behavior. In those early years of your life you'll find and reclaim natural assets that you can use today.

Chapter 4. Work History: Your Skills, Preferences, and Strengths. A clear inventory of your skills based on past achievements is central to developing the best work of your life. But it's not enough to know your skills. Genuine strength comes from understanding your values and preferences—how you prefer to use your skills and for what purposes. In Chapter 4 your best work will be further defined by identifying a combination of personal qualities and the skills you choose to offer to the world.

Chapter 5. Using What You Know to Take Control of Your Career. Our best-work potential is often lost in the expectations, beliefs, and myths that surround us. We can all be led astray or into a career wilderness by the abundance of incorrect or outdated career advice out there. In Chapter 5 we will explore how your self-knowledge, not the voices of advisers, offers a variety of directions you can choose from to control your career (not to mention your life).

Part Two. Strategy: It's About Opportunity

The Strategy section (Chapters 6–10) will focus on communicating your value to those who want or need what you offer:

Chapter 6. The Ah-ha Résumé. Creating a "know thyself" résumé is by far the most powerful tool for managing your career. In Chapter 6 you'll get beyond the constraints of traditional résumés and draw on all aspects of your life to determine the skills you want to offer for your best future work. There will be a moment of awareness when you say about your résumé, "Ah-ha! This is me!" Your résumé will evolve as you continue to understand, identify, and benefit from new opportunities and information.

Chapter 7. What's What Networking. The old "who's who" networking is dead. "What's what" networking is the replacement. In Chapter 7 you'll learn that your increasing clarity can help you identify and meet the people who know what's what. They are the ones who can truly help you understand new directions and possibilities.

Chapter 8. Mapping and Tracking Opportunity. Referral, informational, and job interviews are fundamentally different. Each has specific goals, protocols, and follow-up activities. In Chapter 8 you'll map a strategy to build new opportunities and make informed decisions. Every aspect of your experience—professional, community, personal, and creative—will play a part in making new career visions possible.

Chapter 9. Initiating Appropriate Strategies. You'll need to know when and how to take strategic action. With new opportunities in mind, in Chapter 9 you'll create powerful strategic approaches to connect your best work with the real needs of others.

Chapter 10. Professional Identity and Integrity. Developing a self-aware professional persona can create a legacy of your work over your lifetime. In Chapter 10 you'll focus on workplace cultures and the values at the core of organizations. Once you know how to identify what suits you and what doesn't, you'll be in a position to do your best work and collaborate toward shared visions. Integrity and values will be evident in your work and life activities.

Part Three. Action: It's About Resources

Part Three, Action (Chapters 11–15), will help you explore written and electronic information sources, the growing range of career-related services, and personal and professional networks and events that offer career opportunities. This part of *The Best Work of Your Life* will not give you all the specific information you wish it would. It will do something much better.

Part Three will show you how to target the information you need without drowning in information you don't need. Because we live in the continuous churn of the information age, there is little you can learn about jobs and careers that will not change quickly. You'll be astonished by how much valuable information exists and can be tracked even as it changes.

To demonstrate the ways in which you can learn exactly what you need to know to take strategic action, we provide four case studies. Our fictional characters represent individuals at varied career stages, with different levels of education. Their ages, life stages, and career challenges are unique and contemporary. You'll follow along as each character identifies and discovers information for making an informed career decision. You'll see how they schedule time for research, and you'll also come to understand, as we have, that there are infinite and excellent resources available for those willing to seek them out.

▪ LET'S BEGIN! ▪

This book contains the key principles for lifelong career management. *The Best Work of Your Life* can only happen when you gain clarity, create a strategy, and take action. It's time to start.

Part I
CLARITY

The best work of your life is yet to come. Finding it will depend on gaining a clear understanding of your skills and your values, along with the ways you prefer to work, and developing opportunities for putting all of that together.

Your discovery will begin with a series of steps you'll take to examine your past to uncover personal qualities and talents that you may have overlooked or even forgotten. There may be some surprises as you recall activities you loved as a child, games you invented, or stories you told. You're not out to recapture your childhood, but to reclaim those natural assets that were evident even in your early years.

Next you'll consider your work history and examples of previous "best work" you've done. These may be found in paid work, volunteer work, or life experience. You'll discover in each achievement a quality that will be important to your future success.

By looking at how you like to work and the parameters that constrain your life right now, you'll move into a well-informed present knowing what you'd like to be doing. This isn't easy, but we'll take you through a process that will help clarify it for you.

By the end of the first five chapters, you'll have built a framework for future choices. The strengths you've identified will become the focus of opportunity for your best work. You will have arrived at a powerful present earned by an honest appraisal of the past and a meaningful look to the future. The best work of your life will draw on strengths from your past that you choose to use in the future. This will be the clarity that you'll achieve.

From Current Reality to Career Vision

Times have changed. Really changed. There is no such thing as "a career" as we have known it in the past. You can no longer depend on a steady job with regular promotions at the same company over a prolonged period. The conveyor belt that once hauled employees forward and upward has jerked to a halt, and the floor is littered with casualties. Those left on the belt are barely hanging on.

No wonder the "career advice lines" all have calls waiting. You know you have to *do something*—you may even have an idea or two—but not many people know how to move forward with confidence. Most people are already overwhelmed by the responsibilities in their lives and the perpetual frenzy that seems to be the major sign of our times. If anything, we want to calm down, not rev up.

Today's bookstores are full of job and career books with layers of complicated information and advice and promises for the perfect solution to your career situation, no matter who you are. Many of them were written ten or more years ago and advertise annual "new editions." But in the meantime the workplace has changed and will keep changing. The workplace of today calls for a totally new perspective, not a new edition. Our attitudes about the importance of our personal lives are also shifting. And our needs and interests will continue to vary. An approach that is grounded in simple and flexible principles will enable you to re-create your career as things change, in the world and in your own life.

▪ THREE BASIC PRINCIPLES: CLARITY, STRATEGY, ACTION ▪

Clarity, Strategy, and Action: these are the three principles that will help the *beginner* understand the value to be gained in a first job and to understand when to move on. They will help the *midlife* administrator create a plan to get out of the doldrums and into meaningful work. They will allow someone *five years into the workforce* to create a break—to find a period of temporary work and temporary relief before she becomes cynical and unproductive. They will enable a *new-job seeker* to explore her goals and a new city at the same time. They will help an *eighteen-year-old* go to Alaska to work for a year and enter college with a new level of confidence and maturity. And because most of us will never fully retire, these guiding principles can help us begin to plan now for the best work of our lives as *older workers*. That's why we're confident that Clarity, Strategy, and Action will help *you*.

Who Are You?

Which of the following describes you?

- Desperate job seeker ("Just get me work!")
- Midlife numb bunny ("Didn't I shuffle these papers earlier?")
- Anxious overworker ("Give me two more Tums, and I'll stay an extra hour.")
- Deer in the headlights ("I'd run if only I could see.")
- Forlorn dreamer ("Whatever happened to my fifteen minutes of fame?")
- Size 12 body in a size 6 wet suit ("This feels tight!")
- Perpetual searcher ("Gonna find it . . .")

People in the workforce today experience desperation, boredom, anxiety, confusion, frustration . . . The list could go on: panic, numbness, stress, hypnosis, wistfulness, pain. Faint hope in the face of continuing confusion. People today waste a lot of time trying to figure out "the workplace" in order to figure out how to "fit in."

The only way to come to an understanding of your relationship with work—no matter what your age or stage of life—is first to gain insight about yourself as a worker. You'll notice we said "as a worker." It's important to understand that work is a part of a career and a career is a part of life. The idea is to think of work in relation to your current stage of life. We have full confidence that your life will take on a more meaningful perspective as you attend to the challenges of working well at each stage.

We Know What You're Thinking!

I should just "suck it up and move out smartly." Don't. (This isn't the military. It's your life!)

I'll just think about this tomorrow . . . Stop it. (Frankly, Scarlett, you've got to give a damn.)

Something is bound to come along. Reconsider. (Only *death* is necessarily "bound to come along." And that pays nothing at all and the conditions are terrible.)

Maybe I should go back to school. It's possible. (But you still have to face some choices—and a degree won't guarantee any job.)

I've got to put bread on the table. Yes, you do. (So read fast!)

I hate this job and the pay stinks, but when you're just starting out . . . Okay. We all pay our dues. (But when are you going to take control of your situation?)

There are thousands, even millions, of people out there using excuses for not doing the best work of their lives. You can continue staying in a rut with these attitudes—or you can do something about it.

▪ IT'S ABOUT TIME: YOUR LIFELINE ▪

There is nothing as terrifying as our mortality. And there is nothing more exhilarating than coming to terms with it. Once we admit that our time on this planet is limited, we can begin to take charge of it, indeed to be possessive of it.

One of the tools we'll use throughout the book is a Lifeline. The Lifeline will provide a way for you to look backward and forward as you strive for clarity about who you are, what you have to offer, and where you're going. So take a large sheet of paper and turn it sideways. Draw a long horizontal line with the date of your birth on the far left and the date of your death on the far right. (If you give yourself one hundred years, we'll all feel more cheerful about this.) Now put a mark (*) at your present age. Write "Me/Now" at this point. You should feel a growing sense of what we call "necessary urgency."

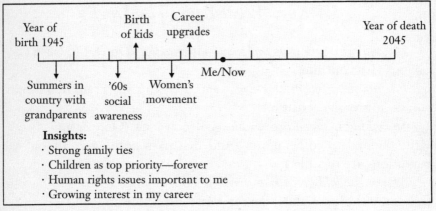

Lifeline: How I've been shaped by the world.

Your "Lasting Marks"

Think back and identify five to ten events in your past that have influenced or shaped your present reality, that have shaped what you believe, what's important to you, what you like or dislike. These may be from your personal life or from work experiences, physical or spiritual, emotional or intellectual, but these events must represent lasting marks or influences on your current reality. Events that have shaped exactly who you are today. Because this chapter is attempting to construct a picture of your current reality, as well as a vision to direct career activity, let's stay with significant events for now, those that have influenced who you are. Events that produce lasting marks might be:

· Summers spent with grandparents
. An award connected with school
· The births or deaths of family members
· Marriages or divorces
· Recognition for special achievements in sports
· Personal bests that others might not know about

Just take ten to fifteen minutes to choose five to ten events that were significant for you in terms of who you are right now. We are all the result of many events that shape us in different ways. The point here is to identify the most important forces along your particular Lifeline. Don't proceed further until you've identified your significant events and marked them along your Lifeline.

Okay, that's the past. And it's very important, because those five to ten events alone have made your Lifeline unique. Those events and all the others over the years have added up, creating who you are right now.

A friend of ours always reminds us, "We're each the stars of our own lives." We would quickly add that we are also the directors of our own lives—unless we've given that power to someone else. If we have, it's time to take it back. And recording your Lifeline is the natural place to start.

You Can See into the Future

Now look to the future. Depending on your age, this part can get scary. A twenty-three-year-old client we met with several years ago became stuck at this point of the exercise. She didn't know her future. We asked her if she ever hoped to marry and have kids. "Sure," she said. So we put a notch at around forty on her Lifeline, a traditional cutoff age for childbearing. Suddenly, the space between twenty-three and forty looked short. She frowned. The reality hit her hard. She was contemplating taking a job working in Antarctica on a recycling project—a demanding job best taken when one is young and strong. This might be the only time in her life to take such a job *and* such a risk to do something unconventional.

She took the job. When she returned a year later, she had a very different perspective on her Lifeline. She had learned so much about environmental issues that she told us her experience had caused her to reconsider the possibility of family and children. "I've learned that there might be many ways to be a part of the future, to add to the planet." Perhaps she'll have had kids by the time she's forty; perhaps she won't. In any case, she has a sense of time and a new perspective on how she might spend that short piece of her Lifeline between now and forty. The notch on the future part of her Lifeline that represented having children might change to represent caring for and nurturing our physical environment. The vision that carried her forward was based on a value that can remain in place while the actions she takes to express it change.

Look at the length of your Lifeline beyond the Me/Now point. This is your future. Try sketching in some goals. (Use a pencil so you'll feel free to change your mind.) What are some of the experiences you want to have in your lifetime? What are your ambitions and aspirations? What dreams can you at least pencil in?

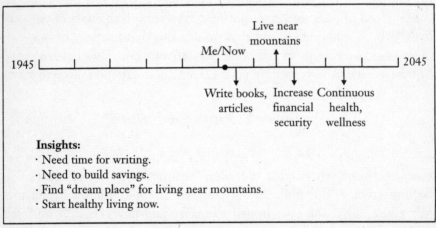

Lifeline: Future goals, dreams, life stages.

Because our focus is going to be on your work life, make notes as you consider ways you might work that will help you reach your goals. If you want to live in Europe, envision getting a job that will take you to Budapest or Prague. If you want to help the homeless, start thinking about programs you'd consider to make this a part of your career. Remember, we are only sketching possibilities here, not making commitments.

For Example . . .

Life *is* short, but it's also wide. You're going to have a lot of things going at the same time. Your goals need to be supported by your work choices. This takes thinking and planning.

Let's try some fairly specific examples of goals you might have.

- Educating your children. Think about what this goal really means in terms of your work and career. Do you want to finance their education, be an active participant as they learn, or help them learn self-sufficiency by financing their own schooling? Your work will have to be high-paying for the first, flexible for the second, and probably a strong, supportive example for the third.
- Building your dream house. Consider your dream house: location, size, cost, style. Where will you work, how much will you need to earn, and when will you find the time to enjoy this house? If it's a serious goal, get it down on paper.
- Running a marathon. You'll want to have the time and discipline, not to mention energy, to get and stay fit. What kind of work will allow you to be this healthy? What workplaces value and reward the kind of person who is a marathoner?
- Caring for your parents. Again, geography and flexibility will be big influences on your work choices if this is one of your goals. Money might also be an important factor. If you're concerned about the difficulty of caring for your parents, you may need a job that is not very stressful.
- Making a few million dollars. Whether you want to live luxuriously or you simply want to ensure your financial security, you'll need a job that pays well. What industries generate lots of money? Big money usually involves taking big chances, so you need to consider your comfort level with risk. (Hint: look backward on your Lifeline. In what ways have you taken risks in your life?)

These are just a few examples—and some thoughts about things that you should consider. Take a few moments to think about each of your goals and the practical considerations involved in each one.

▪ WORKING FOR YOUR LIFE ▪

Whatever your future goals, it's important to understand that your work will need to support your efforts to pursue those goals. Otherwise, you're unlikely to reach them. Even if you're longing to develop a spiritual life and that goal seems entirely disconnected from your career decisions or directions, don't be fooled. It's all connected. It's hard to be cutthroat all day and then be spiritual after five. You'll probably need a job that doesn't require you to be ruthless. If being near your extended family is important, you wouldn't want to seek a job that moves you around the country. Our point here is that getting clear about what you value, what you hope, and what you dream will help you get clear about how you will work.

The goal of your Lifeline exercise is to get you to see the events that have shaped who you are. And to think about where you want to go and how much time you have to get there, so you can shape your work decisions.

Does the length of your future Lifeline make you uncomfortable? Good. It should.

There is a very fine line between taking yourself seriously and taking yourself too seriously. Most of us have a somewhat serious illusion that others are watching us, judging us. Maybe they are, but we need to get over caring too much about other people's opinions when making personal decisions. It seems that many people subconsciously use that concern as an excuse for not being bolder. If you expand your dreams and depart from the straight and narrow of your Lifeline, if you decide to take chances and take control, you'll end up with some peaks and valleys to record in the future. On the other hand, if you walk your Lifeline like a tightrope, most likely no one will notice, but you'll be painfully aware of the tension. It's your choice.

A sense of humor is critical—be able to laugh at yourself. And a sense of urgency is necessary—start living the future now. Look at your Lifeline. You've got some important goals. When are you going to start working toward them? When are you going to develop a vision for your life and your career? As a good friend often says, "If not now, when?"

▪ VISIONS: PAST, PRESENT, FUTURE ▪

A client recently wrote to us, "My needs and goals keep changing. How can I find a personal vision for my overall career when I can't even make sense of my life in these crazy times?"

That's a very good question—and one that bothers a lot of people. It seems that we either take this "vision thing" too seriously or not seriously enough. To create your vision, you need to work with purpose and intention. But you should also realize that we don't get a vision "once and for all." Through self-understanding we identify driving values, events, and preferences that help us create a work life based on our guiding principles. We can't know the purpose of our lives simply by looking either backward or forward. We must also understand and create an *intentional* present—one that we develop consciously. The more we understand about our past and present, the more control we'll have in making necessary changes in the future.

Living "mindfully" in these ways is particularly challenging in our hectic times. Developing a vision means looking both within and outside of ourselves. Our vision helps us achieve our goals, but it also helps us adjust to changes in our environment. Clinging to a vision that cannot adapt is just as bad as having no vision at all.

> **So We Asked an Expert.** Pam Wegner, Vice-President, Information Technology and Administration, Wisconsin Power and Light, states: "Self-knowledge plays a substantial part in the hiring process. People can learn job content but not everyone has the capability for self-knowledge. You can't get far in most jobs if you don't have it."
>
> **The Point:** Self-understanding combines with strategy and action to form an ongoing vision.

A friend once told us this story about her father:

> *My father was a self-made man. Born in 1914, he grew up in Chicago during the Great Depression and managed to learn printing in trade school while working to support his mother and sisters. When he died, in his sixties, he had risen through the ranks of the printing industry from shop work to the corporate suites of international trade. The world during his early career years*

was in postwar economic recovery, and his energy matched the upward surge of opportunity. His temperament was well suited to the printing culture, where good machinery, skilled craftsmen, and continuously developing technology were valued and rewarded. It's easy to look back and understand that a strong management style, a generous view of American culture, and a stubborn adherence to quality standards were important to his career. They were also the values that resulted from his upbringing and from the events of his youth.

Like many men of his era, he took his identity from his work and only softened the edges of who he was later in his life. In time, he volunteered with the Boy Scouts, enjoyed vacations with his grandchildren, and even developed a few spiritual habits near the end. If one could identify his vision or purpose, it was most likely to take advantage of opportunity and provide a better life for his children than he'd had. A workingman's vision in mid-century America.

I don't know if there is a better work vision than the one I learned from my dad—continuous achievement based on continuing ambition for all the right reasons. He knew who he was and what he had to offer, and he understood where in his world to offer it for maximum return. It was a simple equation in simpler times.

ဇ ဇ ဇ

We'll say it again. Times have changed. Values in the workplace have changed. The values of the workforce have changed, too. Experts tell us that people starting to work now will make an average of seven career changes in their lifetimes. A generation ago, a life could be defined in predictable stages: birth, education, marriage, family, work, retirement, and death. Today we understand that education is necessarily a lifelong activity. The gender roles that so defined lives in earlier times are breaking down. Remarriage is nearly as common as marriage and brings with it new or blended families and increased responsibilities. Caregiving of our aging parents matches in duration the number of years we nurture our children. Retirement increasingly brings rehirement, as people leave their careers earlier and then seek next-career phases.

We now have many more opportunities and challenges than the father in the story. But the basic idea behind the "simple equation" holds true—he knew who he was and what he had to offer, and he understood where in his world to offer it for maximum return. For the best work of your life, you need to know yourself, what you have to offer, and where you can offer it for maximum return. But you need to know what that maximum return means for you, and you need to prepare for changes.

America is aging wonderfully well. Not only can we expect to live twenty years longer than our grandparents, but we can anticipate feeling and looking younger. What does that mean for you? Retiring at sixty-five, then spending twenty years in a rocking chair? Being pushed out of your job, to end up working in a fast-food joint? Or simply moving from one phase to another in your life and work? Chances are very good that we'll need and want to work as we age.

Throughout our lifetimes and our careers, there will be times when our priorities shift. Times when we need money more than freedom or time more than money. We will throw over security and stability in favor of flexibility and change at one stage, then return and embrace them at another. There will be no predictable set of priorities, as in generations past. Each life stage will require new ways to work.

▪ KEY VISION INFLUENCES ▪

The only way to develop a vision for our work, then, is to understand and honor the changing priorities in our lives and the need to match our purpose not only to internal values (our personal lives) but to external circumstances (the workplace).

The Changing Workplace

A huge, external consideration is the changing workplace itself. Few companies offer continuing lifetime opportunity and security to employees. In fact, it's ironic that as people become more highly skilled and highly paid, when they should be more valuable to their employers, they're actually more likely to be seen as luxurious resources too expensive to retain.

The much-heralded virtual office has freed companies to find and use human resources swiftly and efficiently without the overhead of space, equipment, or paid employee benefits. Organizational missions shift frequently or are reinterpreted according to changing economic and political realities. And with a global economy connecting the continents, such realities change continuously.

In a recent national leadership conference on workplace and workforce trends it was noted that:

> *The workplace will depend more than ever before on the interpersonal skills of its workers. In fact, the future workplace will stress technological and effective interpersonal skills equally. Significant changes in what employers expect of their employees will include emphasis on empowerment, collaboration, and adapting to new corporate structures. Telecommunications and global competition will speed up workers' days and increase stress. The workforce will be more culturally diverse and contingency workers (contractors, temps, and consultants) will be more common.*
>
> *People in the workforce, as they prepare for the future, will need to focus on their ability to think and solve problems, make decisions with confidence, and communicate effectively. They will be expected to work well (and share credit) with others, yet be accountable and personally responsible. An effective worker will be one who can clarify values, set and attain goals, and engage in continuous learning.*

That's the future of work—and it's happening now. It's overwhelming. How can any of us meet the expectations and demands of this changing world of work? How can we create a necessary vision to propel us into the best work of our lives? How will we find a design within a churning kaleidoscope?

▪ FINDING BALANCE IN THE MIDST OF CHANGE ▪

We believe the only answer is to take control and manage work choices within the context of our lives and within the realities of the workplace. It's important to keep a balance between internal (personal) factors and external (workplace) factors. We must avoid going so far afield with internal preferences that we lose sight of practical options (as in "I've finally discovered the real me! I want to do cat hair weavings"). Neither should we go so far into the analysis of the marketplace that we grab at any job possibility that sounds about right (as in

"Honey, I got the job as a systems analyst. The company's going global! I leave for Romania next week").

The trick, or the art, of doing the best work of our lives is to find clarity about what we have to offer and want to offer, create a strategy to do our best work, and take action to make them fit together. Clarity, Strategy, and Action: we need to find a balance. And that balance will be aided by remembering who we are and how we have been formed by significant events in our lives. We need to use a strong hand in designing the Lifeline that is our future.

Becoming Clear

Sometimes a simple goal arises that offers clarity in our next best work:

- · A high school graduate who comes to understand that continuous learning is as important as salary and benefits when looking for a job will be able to mark her Lifeline with a period of learning and growth.
- · A new college grad sees only a five-year window on his Lifeline to work in an exotic location and combine career with life adventure.
- · A midlife executive recognizes that her peak earning years are in the immediate future and knows that underemployment is not an option. She will have to strive for the biggest challenge possible. Increased financial security will fill the next years on her Lifeline.
- · A working parent craving the option to attend to family will mark flexibility as a value that must be addressed while the children are young.

These are moments of clarity for envisioning next-career decisions. Each is unique and personal, and each is based on individual values that are attached to a particular life stage. People need to create a strategy based on the best available information to find work that helps them achieve their goals.

Clarity and Unfolding Visions

At this point we'd like to share the unfolding of the visions of three clients who, over time, reshaped their careers. Their processes demonstrate what we've been describing. All did considerable work to gain clarity about themselves, their pasts, and their probable future needs and desires. All started with a clearer sense of their present (Me/Now).

Adam had been in the workforce for two years as a middle-school English teacher. Everything fit except that salary levels and advancement possibilities were too limited for his ambitious nature. His department chose him to be chair, so his rapid rise had already taken him to a very real ceiling. He realized, by thoroughly reviewing his Lifeline, that his best achievements and feelings came from his work as a motivational leader and as an effective communicator. He also had strong human relations skills. Adam liked helping others learn. Because the current economy was considered robust, he wondered if there was a setting within the business world in which he might use his best skills and take advantage of higher earning opportunity. Throughout his life, Adam had been energetic and competitive, and he felt he could handle the rigors of a business environment. Where would he begin to explore to match his values, skills, and needs in the marketplace? As he conducted research on career possibilities, Adam found that corporate training was a potential direction. Through a conversation at a community event, he heard about some innovative education programs in several large cities, and he considered a move. Although this discovery was unexpected, Adam created a strategy to explore both directions—corporate training and education programs—as he planned a new vision. His vision was formed by his goals and his self-understanding.

Dora worked for a large corporation in real estate acquisition for ten years. She was a technical expert in her field, highly organized, and able to handle tough decisions. Dora never missed a deadline. But her mother had become frail and was in need of more attention, so Dora was motivated to change career direction to include a more personal vision— being more available to her mother. She had a lot to offer and was willing to scale down her salary expectations. In order to do her best work, Dora required flexibility. She realized that she would likely need to learn about new workplace cultures. She had been in large corporate settings all her professional life, and it would be up to her to tailor her vision for a new setting. The more Dora learned, the more she realized that the marketplace needed her skills. The boom in small-business development interested her, as did the changing face of commercial real estate. Through networking she suspected that state and local economic development agencies in her area might indeed benefit from her corporate perspective and her understanding of how to conduct business transactions efficiently. These were the areas Dora strategically explored. Dora's vision was marked by her desire to care for her mother. This change was driven by her values and the decline in her mother's health. Her talents would support her deeply personal goal. Her Lifeline reflected a rich and changing vision for the near future.

Jackie, a hospital-based nurse for five years, was convinced she'd chosen the wrong profession. The frustrations she felt due to the frenzy and pressures at work had begun to make her literally sick. The health care system she entered had changed, and this was not what she bargained for. The values she prized in becoming a nurse were no longer central in her work setting, and it hurt. She was afraid she was getting an ulcer. Jackie knew her patterns of achievement and her inherent skills quite well. She cared deeply about people, was detail-oriented, and was able to help others most by explaining health issues with sensitivity and compassion. She was strongly motivated to reach out to the increasing numbers of aging people who were living alone and dealing with complex medical needs. She had been painfully aware of the need for such care in the past few years in her industry. To help people in this way, she would have to be able to spend time with patients to understand and attend to the details of their lives. This would never happen in her current workplace. As Jackie began to search out new career options, she found that the marketplace was, indeed, beginning to develop services for elderly people. She could use her skills working in home health care agencies, employee assistance programs, or the new facilities being developed for an increasingly aging population. Jackie spent time exploring each of these new possibilities. She saw a change in her industry and an opportunity for a new career vision. She brought the skills and values from her past straight into her future not only with clarity but with greater possibility for meaningful achievement.

Your Vision Is Unique

There are few career visions that are "automatic" or "programmed," immediately apparent from our education or training. Even among professionals (doctors, lawyers, engineers) or skilled workers (mechanics, masons, plumbers) there are many choices for those who care to sort out the personal version of their careers. The combination you must seek is the matrix of: skills you offer, marketplace needs, and the manner of working that fits your values and life stage.

One of our favorite clients is an eighty-three-year-old friend who recently asked us to help her return to her career after a period of physical rehabilitation. Her vision of getting back to work is not the usual octogenarian's priority. On the other hand, we've seen dozens of people in their twenties and early thirties who would seem almost to be seeking a "retirement" lifestyle—one that allows them freedom to study and explore the world, to seek pleasure and adventure. Such visions are a possible reality once you understand how to frame a step-by-step approach to move forward. But the strategy must be built on self-understanding before you take the first step.

Acknowledging our life stages gives us tremendous insight about what is possible. Consider the following three examples, as related by a friend:

> In my current career phase, I love to travel, write, and create projects for large companies. I'm an "empty-nester." There's no way I could have or would have worked in this way when my kids were still around.
>
> My youngest daughter works in the fast-paced film industry in Hollywood. Her energy and her earnings are high, and it's important to her to enjoy her creative circle of friends while she's still young and single. She's aware of how limited this time will be.
>
> My older daughter has recently taken a brief time-out from her six-year career to be close to her two small half sisters. She sees this as a unique opportunity to reclarify career direction, bond with the little ones, and plan

a strategy to work in New York City next. Her temporary summer job in the Midwest supports her interim vision quite well.

ᘓ ᘓ ᘓ

So We Asked an Expert. Linda Bohman, Human Resources Director, Virchow Krause and Co., relates: "Past behaviors are my strongest indication of future behaviors. That's a personnel professional's best indicator. Use their history to predict the future pattern of longevity and performance."

The Point: The better you understand your history, the better you can position yourself in an interview.

These are just three examples. Each of our Lifelines is marked by specific opportunities that are time-limited and unique.

Your current reality is the stepping-off place toward your future vision. Your vision will not be fully formed, because every two or three steps we take help us retool and revise our future plans, hopes, and dreams. But your vision can begin to be anchored in the reality of your past and the probability of your future. Those Lifeline events that created lasting marks will help you know what to strive for. In addition, the life stages from your past and the life stages you anticipate for the future can also help you sketch some new goals and directions.

This is just a beginning. In the following chapters you will look deeper into the past to add to your future possibilities. With genuine clarity about who you are, what is possible about the future in terms of your circumstances and your goals, you will begin to identify the best work of your life.

ACTION STEPS TO FORM YOUR VISION

1. What three events in your past have influenced you most? (Focus on three.) What are the results in terms of who you are right now? Write down how you felt, what you learned, or whatever made these three events those that you consider the most influential.
2. What life stages do you anticipate in the next ten years? Marriage? Children? Education? Caregiving? How will your life stage changes affect the way you can or will work? Income needs? Location changes? Flexibility requirements? Write down life

stages and changes you anticipate, as if recording the history of your next ten years.

3. Read over the classified ads of a recent Sunday newspaper. With pen in hand, move quickly through the ads and mark a "Y" or an "N" (for "yes" or "no") to indicate your immediate reaction to a job. Skip the ones that provoke an ambivalent response. Then go back through, considering the ads one by one. What personal characteristics caused you to give an immediate yes or no to a job description? Take two sheets of paper, labeling one "Yes" and the other "No." For each ad, list your reasons on the appropriate sheet.

4. Now review your two lists. On another sheet, list the qualities of the jobs you marked with a "Y." List the qualities of an "N" job. How do these relate to your personal qualities? What intrigues you? Repulses you?

5. Make sure your Lifeline is as complete as possible for the focus of this chapter. Past events and probable future events should be noted, as these events have influenced or will influence who you are. Give notice to the spot that identifies Me/Now. From current reality to ultimate vision is only a series of steps, and they start from exactly where you are at this moment.

6. Collect your thoughts and insights in a notebook under a section marked "Gaining Clarity." What have you learned about yourself through reading this chapter?

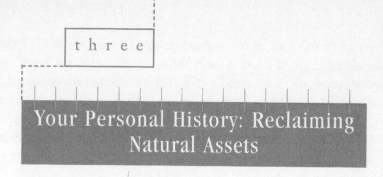

three

Your Personal History: Reclaiming Natural Assets

This year's Lifetime Achievement Award winner in our community surprised banquet guests by accepting the honor with pride rather than false humility. In his after-dinner speech, community leader Harold Carver forewent the usual flattering and bowing to those honoring him. Instead, with simple dignity he accepted recognition for his achievements.

"I'm grateful for the opportunities that have lit the path," he said, "but I've been on the path for as long as I can remember." He recalled his early childhood tendency toward philanthropy when he collected money for local flood victims. He described the continuous patterns of setting difficult goals and tenaciously reaching them in elementary school, high school, college, and as an adult. "I've always been sensitive to the injustices and hardships of others, and I learned throughout my lifetime to put those feelings to work. My achievements—part nature, part nurture, part opportunity—are no accident. I've simply tried to know who I am and to be of use to the world."

▪ BEING A CONTRIBUTOR ▪

"To be of use." That simple phrase is one of the most meaningful experiences we can have in our lives. Yet it is not a simple task to know ourselves well enough to be truly useful.

Experts cite recognition as the highest reward we can get from our work (almost always ranked above salary). And yet, to be of use, to do work worthy of recognition, we need a very real understanding of our unique human nature. Notice the priority in that final statement by Harold Carver: "I've simply tried *to know who I am* and to be of use to the world."

We need to recognize who we are. Without genuine self-recognition, we're very likely to become alienated. When we've lost the commitment to being who we really are, we end up:

- Working over our heads
- Underemployed
- Bored
- Feeling pushed and exhausted by meaningless goals
- Feeling like impostors
- Promising anything others ask and losing more of what we could genuinely offer

It's important to look backward to understand the future. Look back through your life for patterns of accomplishments based on your nature and opportunities that express your best qualities and characteristics. Try to identify, from earliest stories or memories, the way you did things, the "youness" in your achievements, what makes you unique. Let's look at some examples of what we mean, people whose childhood interests and abilities are very much a part of their present and future.

A little boy we knew began and grew a comic book collection until it numbered thousands of copies. He sorted and organized his collection meticulously. An unusually self-reliant child, he spent hours in his room and seemed to crave solitude even though he had a lively group of friends, played on sports teams, and eventually held an after-school job. He is now in his mid-fifties, and, although he has a successful career in which he manages many people, he still maintains a special hobby. In the free hours he has between dinner and sleep, he enjoys working diligently on a literary bibliography based on adventure tales. His office is his haven, lined floor-to-ceiling with shelves of books. He is, as he was nearly fifty years ago, focused, organized, and lost in adventures.

A friend with a very successful retail store and catalog mail-order enterprise makes her living in the business of whimsy, nostalgia, and dreams. She fills her life, and her customers' lives, with collections of 1950s memorabilia, hilarious novelty items, original lamps, and furnishings for the not-so-serious homemaker. Everything is meant to delight. Her annual Spam-carving contest raises money for local Seattle charities. On the back of her store's catalog and throughout the store itself are pictures of her— Ruby Montana, aged five, sitting on a pinto pony, her big brown eyes unblinking under the brim of her Dale Evans cowgirl hat. She says, "I never got that pinto pony. It came through our neighborhood in Oklahoma with a photographer. But I promised myself that someday, when I made my best dream come true, I'd remember that moment." Her store is called Ruby Montana's Pinto Pony. Every day is a good ride for Ruby. She brought that little girl along every step of the way throughout her career.

These two people have found happiness in something from their childhood that they've kept within them and around them throughout their lives. The moral of the stories: know who you are and how it can help you be of use to the world.

> **So We Asked an Expert**
> K. Dean Moore, Director of Human Resources, Kodak Colorado Division, Eastman Kodak Co., says: "We get into someone's personal nature by having them do a lot of reflecting back, not predicting forward. This is the way we try to get information on personal styles."
>
> **The Point:** Be prepared to talk about your natural assets and personal perspectives as a part of what you offer.

▪ LOOK FOR THE SIMPLEST STORIES, THE ONES THAT REMIND YOU WHO YOU ARE ▪

When we read biographies of famous people, the authors often point out how aspects of the subject's later ambitions and abilities, loves and hates, virtues and vices, can be found in his or her earliest childhood. Well, famous folks are no different from the rest of us, in that respect at least. Try thinking about yourself from a biographer's perspective. Where can you find evidence of who you are? Just look for the simplest stories.

We know a highly successful scientist who didn't speak a word until he was nearly two years old. He then surprised his mother by asking, "Is dinner ready, honey?" This toddler's method of observing his father, thinking and rehearsing his thoughts carefully before ever speaking a word, is characteristic of his adult scientific behavior—observe, collect data, analyze, speak.

A minister who continues to lead and inspire others well into his retirement recalls early yearnings to help others. He also describes himself as having been a cherished only child who adored the limelight but had to work hard to meet his parents' expectations. His continuing vocation is no mystery. It seems deeply rooted in several facets of his identity. His habit of helping and inspiring others is made unusually generous when combined with his strong work ethic.

When you're trying to figure out how to do the best work of your life, what moved you as a child still has relevance today. So let's explore that some more.

▪ THINK BACK WITH AFFECTION ▪

In this section, we're going to help you (re)construct your Lifeline. To guide you, we've listed some questions. You may either answer them one by one or read them all, then answer the ones that seem most meaningful to you. The point is to mark your Lifeline with your most important memories that show you developing into who you are now.

Think over your life as far back as possible. What stories or incidents do others in your family tell about you as a young child? What are the earliest signs you can remember of who you are now? Don't try to analyze yet. Just try to remember and to gather your history in this way.

Again, draw your Lifeline, one hundred years long. Put the Me/Now spot on the line.

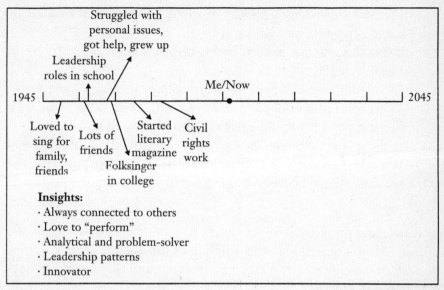

Lifeline: Personal history/natural assets.

Focus backward now through your earliest years, before the age of five. Note along your Lifeline stories and incidents and what they reveal about your nature from the very beginning. When you were very small, what were you like?

- Did you play industriously by yourself?
- Did you terrify your parents by climbing up onto the backs of chairs and leaping into space?
- Did you stand in the center of family gatherings and sing or dance?
- Did you wander away from home and create a real-life drama?
- Did you sit on a neighbor's front porch swing and tell all your family's secrets?
- Did you make other children laugh? Did you make them cry?

Think next about your early school years—when you were five to ten years old. Add additional notes to your Lifeline as you remember incidents and characteristics.

- How did you react to going to school? Did you take to it easily or reluctantly?

· Did you establish a personal relationship with your teachers or try to disappear into the crowd?
· What role did you take at recess or playtime? Leader, follower, joiner, rebel?
· Were you competitive in the classroom or in sports activities?
· What sorts of kids liked to hang out with you? Why?
· What moments in your early childhood allowed you to shine? A spelling bee? A role in the school play? Befriending someone you felt was less fortunate than you? Being chosen to help the teacher? Creating classroom hilarity by mimicking the principal?

And now think back to the time when you were between ten and fifteen. Make notes along your Lifeline of the qualities that continue to surface through events. What new interests and characteristics were beginning to emerge?

· What kinds of relationships were you developing at school, at home, in your neighborhood?
· Did you take care of younger siblings or neighborhood children?
· Did you engage in extracurricular activities at school?
· Was accepting responsibility from teachers or parents a joy or a burden?
· Did you rebel? If so, in what ways? If not, what did you think of those who did?
· How did you feel about the behavior of your peers? Why?
· Whom did you admire? Movie stars? Musicians? World leaders? School "personalities"?
· What ideas did you have about what you wanted to be when you grew up?
· What were your highest hopes for yourself?
· What were your biggest fears?
· How did you feel about your future?

Between the ages of fifteen and twenty, how did your life change? These years mark a transition to independence and can provide rich insights into why we are who we are now. Continue adding notes to your Lifeline for this period. You will begin to see yourself as you are now, with qualities and characteristics rooted in your earlier years and evident in your interests and activities.

· How well did you feel you fit into the world?
· How would your best friend from that time describe you?
· What were you known for in high school?
· How were you described in your yearbook? The "one most likely to" what? If your yearbook didn't do such descriptions, how do you think your classmates would have labeled you "most likely"?
· What were your secret wishes, desires, fears? What happened to them?
· When you had to make important decisions—work, college, financial support, living arrangements—how did you make them? Through careful reasoning and research? On impulse? Independently? By discussing the decision with your parents, friends, and teachers?
· What kind of social circles were you in? What role did you take?
· As you began to form adult friendships, who were the people you were drawn to?
· What did you give and get in those relationships?

We hope that these questions have helped you think about your life. If we've triggered a cascade of memories, all the better. What we're trying for here is a recognition of: "Yes, this is me. I've been like this from day one!" Or "Oh! I'd forgotten that I started getting interested in that in my early teens." What are the qualities and characteristics that have been constant in your life? What we're also trying for, however, are responses like:

· I'd completely forgotten how much I used to care about _____.
· I guess I've been _____ for longer than I'd realized.
· Wow! My tendency to _____ has created a lot of similar struggles in my life.
· I wish I could feel the way I did when I _____.

· When I've made decisions in my life, I've usually been
_____.

At this point in thinking about your early years, you should be able to begin listing childhood talents and patterns of behavior. Discovering the qualities you were born with or those that emerged early in your life is an important step. In the following chapters we'll deal with acquired skills and preferences that have surfaced in your work experience. For now, concentrate on the uniqueness of your personal nature and the qualities you've had from the earliest years of your life.

Keep at It

Keep working to distinguish the "youness" that arises out of your history. A good way to do this is by thinking about the milestones that mark the first twenty years for most people, the usual experiences that most of us go through, then looking at the ways in which each was different for you, unique.

Take, for example, learning to ride a bicycle. Did you struggle to keep at it in spite of scraped knees and shins until you triumphed? Or did you fall once or twice, then enlist every adult in sight to help you learn to ride with less risk and a growing sense of group accomplishment? What distinguished your early bicycle-riding experiences?

Think back with wisdom and affection. Sort through the memories of each phase of your early life and identify talents and behaviors, large and small, that offer you a positive sense of who you were, who you still are.

We are mining your past in search of patterns, qualities that became apparent in your activities and reactions to experiences, characteristics that marked moments in your life as unique. We're looking for those gold nuggets—the forgotten favorite moments—so that you might retrieve certain qualities that have been pushed aside in your current life. They could be useful to your future. Make a list of your discoveries as they arise. Don't worry about how you structure your list—or even whether it's a list at all. The point here is to record anything from your past that tells something about who you are: significant events, interests, activities, concerns, hopes, qualities, characteristics.

▪ ESSENTIAL QUALITIES: A CLOSER LOOK AT TWO THAT ARE CRITICAL FOR SUCCESS ▪

Your past reveals patterns that will inform your future. Now that you've dug up memories and recorded them chronologically along your Lifeline, let's narrow our attention to focus on two factors that are critical to the successful achievement of nearly every goal: enthusiasm and good human relations.

These also happen to be the qualities critical to workplace success, according to everyone who's ever been on a hiring committee. A key point to remember here is that it's your particular version of genuine enthusiasm and successful human relations you must identify in order to add these to your personal competencies. Imagine being on a hiring committee and facing a job candidate who shows evidence of these important qualities only to reveal later that he was pretending. Both parties lose.

A friend remembers hiring a man who displayed a good sense of humor during the interviewing process. His technical skills were perfect for the requirements, and his seemingly good-natured personality clinched the deal. He got the job. But, in fact, he was a crabby, cynical, miserable employee. He appeared to do his work, but when others asked for his help, he acted put-upon and was rarely willing to collaborate. His good humor had been a convincing act. It took many months finally to be rid of him, and his time in that position did neither him nor the company any good.

Enthusiasm

Whether you are an extrovert or an introvert, there will be examples on your Lifeline of experiences you were excited about. This is the time to remember those experiences and to consider the causes and conditions that generated positive energy. Remembering and noting your most enthusiastic reactions to earlier life events and your more passionate interests will provide a key for future visions of work that will excite you. And that excitement comes in many styles. Consider the following two people.

Amelia, a research librarian, had a number of other careers before finding her greatest enthusiasm in her current role. She worked in business early on and then was the head of shipping for a large export firm. She even attempted a new career in land surveying at one time. In each of the jobs she was able to use some of her best, natural qualities: detailed management of information and an ability to handle demanding systems and protocols. Her current career as a research librarian, however, engenders genuine enthusiasm and is the best match for her nature and background. A focused and reserved person, she is able to work with detailed systems while serving a small number of courteous patrons in a quiet setting. The deadlines and pressures of previous career phases are gone, as well as the anxiety of working in a competitive setting. She is pleased with herself and her career. The child who loved books can now systematically satisfy her unending curiosity in her work at the reference desk each day.

Not everyone is quietly enthusiastic. Amanda calls frequently to update her mother about her work as a Hollywood publicist. Her family jokes about Amanda's boundless energy. Every day seems to be the best day of her life so far. When she's deflated, she is completely undone, but she recovers fast and seeks challenges that keep her enthusiasm at a higher level than most of us experience. Her Lifeline is full of patterns that predicted her need to work in an extroverted, fast-paced setting. As a child, Amanda composed a poem as she looked at a map of the United States and described all the places she had gone "so far." The "so far" is a key element of her nature. Every day she pushes herself farther. And every day is her best as long as it gets her someplace new. She's crestfallen when she's stuck and immobilized.

So We Asked an Expert. Ellen E. Wood, Human Resources Coordinator, Grant Thornton, LLP, International, notes: "Exceptional employees are usually people who are energetic, enthusiastic, and lively in the interview. They have good interpersonal skills, eye contact, a smiling face, and they are not afraid to tell about failures."

The Point: Professionals value sincere people with genuine vitality and self-understanding.

To know who you are, discover who you used to be. Understanding the child helps you understand the adult and provides clear guidelines for finding the best work of your life.

Human Relations

Good human relations are a basic requirement for successful work. Most jobs involve some need for good "people skills," the ability to "work and play well with others." Yet how we relate to others is highly personal and peculiar to each of us.

We remember, with some affection, a client from several years ago. Jim had worked in the trucking industry as a scheduler and was accustomed to conflict and tough talk as a workplace reality. His outside interests were literally outside. Hunting for bear. Fishing in Montana. He rarely smiled. The only glimmer of enthusiasm he displayed with us, even after several meetings, was a wry grin when he described an upcoming hunting trip.

Meanwhile, Jim had been taking courses and was trying to become a professional in the field of human resources as a next career move. Human resources? We were concerned. How could a man who couldn't smile ever work in a world of selecting, managing, and supporting others.

One day we sat face-to-face in uncomfortable silence. We had been trying to "coach" Jim about increasing his enthusiasm, about connecting more strongly with others, even smiling. He remained stone-faced. We became exasperated.

"Jim," one of us asked, "what are you thinking about these things we're trying to tell you—to be more enthusiastic, to smile?"

He answered, "I think it's bull——."

At least he was frank! Pat looked him straight in the eye and responded, "I think your tough, unsmiling attitude is bull——, too."

Jim grinned. The most animated expression we'd seen so far.

Pat's extroverted, enthusiastic style had caused him to mistrust what she was saying in previous sessions. But his strong and silent demeanor was just as suspect to us. We all realized at that moment that we had a common ground. No bull——!

Jim was able to hear us from that moment on, and we were better able to respect his manner of human relations. When he phoned to update us on his job search progress, Pat was even able to kid him about "smiling" into the phone. And she could tell when he did. Jim landed a good job at a university in human resources in due time. We haven't seen him in several years, but we can picture him working in a no-bull—— way with people, and we hope his no-nonsense nature has added value to the human resources department.

▪ BE TRUE TO YOURSELF ▪

We've all met people who have a canned, impersonal, or insincere version of either enthusiasm or "people skills." We strongly encourage clients to honor their personal nature when showing real enthusiasm and to find their own way of dealing with others. Advice that suggests you cultivate false characteristics for your career is misleading. It implies that phoniness is acceptable and that others will be fooled if you "act" enthusiastic. They might be, but not for long. Developing the art of getting along with others as well as discovering the sources of your enthusiasm will be a part of the best work of your life. Faking it will create fake situations—and fake expectations and pressures.

Picture the grinning guy who, when asked "How are you?" replies "Great! And getting better!!" Perhaps he's being sincere, but we would believe that response only from somebody trying to sell us something. It doesn't ring true in ordinary life. Try finding and expressing enthusiasm in a personal, nonclichéd way. Be specific. Be you.

Maria is the head of our local county cultural commission. She makes a lot of people happy awarding grants for local performers and artists. Although the selection process is a challenge, Maria has unflagging enthusiasm for her work and impeccable interpersonal skills. Whatever events shaped Maria's childhood and developed her nature must have included positive and lasting success with people. You can't fake it.

So you have to have enthusiasm to work well, and you have to be able to relate well to people. Frequently, the two are connected, but not always. Some people are more enthusiastic about a successful collaboration, others about projects accomplished alone. What is important is to identify instances of enthusiasm and instances of good human relations skills. Then you can begin to draw on those experiences to re-create the circumstances necessary to do the best work of your life.

Think through your past and identify the times you were truly enthusiastic. Pay attention to whether those times were alone or shared with others.

Things that generate solo excitement might be:

· Starting a collection of some kind
· Mastering the trombone or piano
· Participating in individual sports
· Indulging a passion for motorcycles or cars
· Writing stories or poems

On your Lifeline mark those times with an "E" for enthusiasm. It's probably tough to label events in your life so simplistically. But if you think about them, if you go back in time to relive the specifics, it should be easier. If your Lifeline's getting crowded, that's fine. Or draw a separate one to identify these key elements of your past.

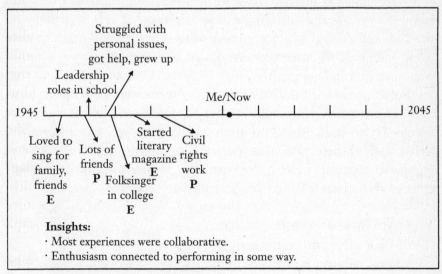

Lifeline: E=enthusiasm, P=people-related.

Now try to recall the times you enjoyed working with others. Mark your Lifeline with a capital "P" for experiences you excelled at while enjoying personal success with other people. What were the conditions that generated this "best self" with others? Don't limit your reflection to work or job experiences. Some examples we've heard as people remember their best work with others are:

· Planting a community garden
· Working on human rights issues
· Competing for a baseball trophy
· Writing a team term paper in school
· Playing in a rock band
· Living cooperatively in student housing
· Working the night shift in a factory
· Remodeling a house
· Driving cross-country with a friend
· Dealing with a family crisis

Each of these activities brought out the best in someone. What about you? Think back as far as you can remember about the times you were engaged in an activity with others. And think of times you enjoyed a private and satisfying experience alone. There is virtually no work we can do that will not involve others, but it's important to note from your past whether you are drawn to collaboration or whether you work best independently.

Focus on three of the experiences that generated genuine enthusiasm. Times when you couldn't wait to get back to what you were doing. Try to relive those moments. Why were you so enthusiastic? What made those experiences special? Don't try to answer the following questions until you've had a chance to ponder and enjoy the memories of those times. When you're ready, ask yourself:

· Was there a vision?
· What values drove the vision?
· How did you feel (hour by hour) as you worked toward your goal?
· What role did you take if others were involved?
· What stories do you remember about people involved in the effort and how they worked?

· What would they remember about you?
· If you were working alone, what did the people around you observe about your work?
· What makes you count this experience among your best?

Now you're beginning to harvest the qualities about yourself that will be important as you strive for work-related clarity. In your past we've been looking for patterns of activity based on your personal nature. We've begun noting the qualities that have developed because of who you are uniquely.

Some people find it difficult at first to think about their past, to reflect on their feelings and interests, to consider how they developed. But we assure you that the results of self-discovery are worth the effort. We urge you to continue through the next steps at any level that is comfortable. Just don't jump to the Strategy part of the book without gaining Clarity.

ACTION STEPS TO REGAIN
YOUR PERSONAL HISTORY

1. Look at the notes you've made and try to summarize by completing this sentence. Don't strain. Trust your ability to draw easily on your past.
   Throughout my life I've been able to get important things done by_____
   _____
   _____.

2. Think about the times you worked with enthusiasm and with strong and successful human relations. Complete these thoughts:
   The best experiences I've had with other people were when I
   _____
   _____.
   And when they_____
   _____.

And together we accomplished_____

_____.

I prefer to work alone when _____

_____.

3. As you contemplate the ways you would like to work in the future,
    remember the times you worked best in the past. Complete this
    thought:
    I'd love to recapture the spirit of the times when _____

    _____.

4. Make a brief summary about each E and each P that you noted on
    your Lifeline. You can recapture the spirit of past successes and
    times of shared accomplishment. If this exercise causes you to feel
    a pleasant nostalgia, pay attention to that. You are the star of your
    own life. Think about creating a situation that will allow you to
    work enthusiastically alone or with others in the future.
5. Collect your thoughts and insights in a notebook under a section
    marked "Gaining Clarity."

Work History: Your Skills, Preferences, and Strengths

*"I always wanted to be somebody. Now I
realize I should have been more specific."*

—LILY TOMLIN

▪ EXPLORING YOUR WORK HISTORY ▪

Consider this story told by a former participant in one of
our workshops:

> *I wanted to be something, be somebody. Like many people, I
> thought I knew my skills and strengths, but I didn't put the clues
> in my work history together until I was in such career discom-
> fort my choice was either get clear or stay miserable. So I looked
> backward with greater focus. I could see that my interest in
> music, math, and language from earliest childhood demonstrated
> a desire for orderly learning and detailed systems. The fact that
> I was the only girl in the science club and that I spent hours alone
> reading and thinking filled in a picture of an independent, quiet
> spirit.*
>
> *So why did my first official job as a speech pathologist cause
> such discomfort? And why did the rewards of my Ph.D. degree
> years later—teaching in a large university—make me feel
> unhappy? The years of disciplined study and research were pure
> pleasure, but the application of my skills within institutions
> trapped and confused my independent spirit and forced me into a
> daily onslaught of human relations that left me no privacy, no
> quiet for my mind and soul. I felt desperate. Trapped. And in the
> end, seriously depressed.*
>
> *Once I began to go more deeply into my work history, I was
> able to pull out the parts of each job I truly enjoyed. I identified*

my past successes in the midst of (in spite of!) miserable jobs, and I stopped blaming myself for not "fitting in." Most important, I began to plan my next career phase in a way that would utilize my best skills in research, study, writing, and teaching in ways that I preferred and that were less conventional, less institutional. I gained a clearer understanding of my work future that not only made sense but created excitement for me.

There is no right age or stage for beginning to explore your work history. As we've seen in previous chapters, our qualities are evident in earliest childhood and are woven throughout our work experience. Perhaps more difficult and more unusual, though, is the task of looking at our past to sort out our *achievements* and our *preferences*, our *natural enthusiasms* and those *unexpected revelations* that help us understand how we can do our very best work.

▪ JOB AND WORK HISTORY: THE DO'S AND DON'TS FOR FUTURE PLANNING ▪

Most of our earliest work experience isn't based on professional skills. We become baby-sitters, stock suppliers, clerks, or fast-food workers to earn money. We learn specific skills such as company procedures or special child care rituals. We also learn general skills like punctuality, time management, customer relations, and organizing and improving systems. We experience jobs we like and jobs we don't. Later, we might sort out valuable new directions based on understanding good and bad work experiences and the things that make them so.

In our work with students, we are fond of reminding them that their academic achievements and credentials are going to provide only one line on their résumé. Similarly, the jobs we have held, the chronological history of our work, is only one piece of the puzzle. Job histories and academic degrees are only useful when you can find the "you" in them. The worst résumés are those that list companies and jobs with "obituary style" birth and death dates, as if the years were more important than the person.

Our focus here is not on résumé formats (we'll deal with that later). Instead, the point is that they should reflect who you really are and what you can contribute. When we look at standard résumés of our older clients, we find they are frequently mired in professional jargon and burdened with detailed chronologies of job histories that wouldn't even interest a doting mother. What you want is a way to find out what makes you a special and potentially valuable candidate for a job. And that does not come from a dry recitation of when you worked where. Discovering your personal vitality is the best way to enliven your résumé and your career.

▪ *HOW*, NOT WHERE OR HOW LONG, YOU'VE WORKED ▪

As a first step, let's systematically examine all the jobs you've had in order to identify the times when your best work stands out. Here are some questions to start the process: When was your personal vitality most engaged in an accomplishment? Which achievements, outside of your formal jobs, do you prize as lifetime accomplishments?

Again, create a hundred-year Lifeline. (Use a larger piece of paper if you prefer.) Mark the Me/Now spot.

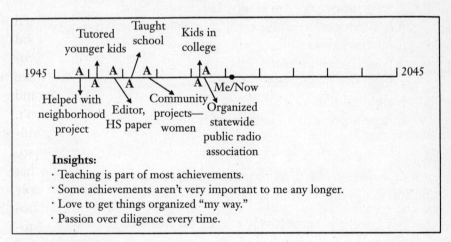

Lifeline: Achievements.

In previous chapters you've identified key events, milestones, behaviors, and patterns of earliest natural work-related identity factors. You've noted the times you were exceptionally enthusiastic (E) and the times you connected meaningfully and successfully with other people (P). This time you will focus on your achievements:

· Something you accomplished
· Something you enjoyed doing
· Something that had real results

Try using five-year blocks from your past. Write an "A" on your Lifeline for each achievement you select. Some achievements may have occurred in work settings, some may have come in extracurricular or volunteer activities, and others may be personal accomplishments achieved privately, within your family or as a solo challenge. The achievements you select should not be hard to identify. They should stand out to you as sources of pride.

Such achievements could include experiences outside the workplace. They might be somewhat varied in the time they took and the role you played. Include accomplishments that make you feel good about your life. To help trigger your memory, here are some examples we've heard from clients.

· A long canoe trip you planned and completed
· A holiday festival you spearheaded that resulted in money raised for a charity
· A language you learned
· Long-term involvement in a neighborhood project
· Helping others work well
· A degree you earned and paid for yourself

Employment-based achievements will be more personal and specific and could include times you:

· Set goals and aggressively met or exceeded them
· Created a new project, a program, or even a department
· Solved a crisis or a problem at work
· Created or found a new resource to help others work better
· Helped improve technical, information, or people-related systems in the workplace
· Increased your expertise or skills and applied your new knowledge for success

· Sought or accepted greater responsibility and increased your value to others

Look back on your Lifeline for the times you worked especially well. What characterizes the achievements you feel best about? These characteristics will become features of your best work and will be part of your future success.

List at least five of the work-related achievements you marked on your Lifeline. Include nonjob achievements if you wish. Next to each, note the skills and strengths that created your success.

ACHIEVEMENTS	BEST-WORK SKILLS AND STRENGTHS
1. Created work/study program for a fine arts school.	Network building, resource development
2.	
3.	
4.	
5.	

As you look at the words you've used to describe your skills and strengths, begin to think of them as personal "gifts" you have used in the world to create success. A great musician has a musical gift. What you feel you do well is your gift. That's what we're looking for here. These are your key *best-work factors*. These are skills you will be able to market effectively to potential employers, particularly if you identify how these skills can help you contribute to an employer's success. The more you can underscore your unique strengths and how those strengths can help others, the more others will be able to recognize your value.

What skills and strengths show up repeatedly on your Lifeline? Are you organized, disciplined, enduring, strong, analytical, or creative? Have you managed people or projects, communicated effectively, motivated others, planned well, researched thoroughly, or improved systems? Think about this carefully while creating your list of achievements and the skills they required.

▪ FOCUSING SYSTEMATICALLY ON YOUR ACHIEVEMENTS AND SKILLS ▪

There is good reason to reflect on your achievements and skills before rushing to apply for any old job or make new decisions about your career. As people move from job to job, they are rarely in control of the direction they are going. It would be unusual for a young person to say, "Before I make any career move, I'm going to make sure I really understand my basic qualities and skills." In fact, it's even unusual for a midlife professional to move forward with such insight or control. More commonly, people move forward based on the needs of an employer, what they perceive as needs in the marketplace, or chance. Our goal here is to help you avoid that by helping you take control of your career. By understanding what you're really good at, what your gifts are, you can be proactive in identifying opportunities and taking advantage of them.

Sometimes we've found that aptitude tests and counselors give people absurdly wrong guidance. One client of ours told of taking a skills and preferences test and being advised to become a graveyard worker. The test he had taken found that he loved nature and was a compassionate person. A preprogrammed analysis created a big future for him in the cemetery business. On the other hand, an old friend of ours is, in fact, a cemetery keeper and has found great satisfaction in the beauty, spirituality, and compassionate human relations that make up his day-to-day job.

Career-related tests and analyses can help suggest patterns and possibilities, but no one knows better than you what you would really like to do. You can become an expert on yourself by taking the time to sort out your experiences. Once you get into the habit of sorting and clarifying events in your life, your ability to influence and control how you work will increase dramatically. Why is this? Because you'll be operating from a position of strength and certainty about yourself and clarity about what you can do.

It's all up to you. Your company or organization is not in the business of building your career. Job listings or classified ads are not printed to offer you self-fulfillment. It is your responsibility to develop and maintain your career. And remember, if you don't take the time to do it, you'll find that it's easy to get yourself off track.

A colleague told us her story:

> *I have long understood about myself that I love words, causes, and people, and I like creating motivation by bringing them together. And yet at one time in my career, I found myself managing a huge direct-mail marketing department for a major university. The department used words and causes to motivate people, but I became increasingly distanced from my best skills and strongest preferences. I was, instead, buried in printing schedules, cost analyses, postal regulations, paper pricing, and spreadsheets with thousands of numbers that represented the response rates of human beings but had little to do with speaking to them directly.*
>
> *How did I get to such a level of discomfort and so far away from the values that inspire me and the skills that are my strongest? A big promotion, that's how. Worse still, I'd even asked for the promotion.*
>
> *It was a promotion that moved me up but away from my source of personal vitality. Only after spending two years in my new position did I admit that I hated my day-to-day tasks and was at a level of extreme dissatisfaction. Yet I had risen to the position and was able to do the job well. The department's goals were being achieved, I was being paid more than ever, but my best skills were lost in the process.*
>
> *Increasingly, I sought projects outside of my job that took me back to working with people and with words. I volunteered as a political strategist for local candidates, I met with students to help them write résumés and plan career strategies, I signed on for a civic project that required a two-year public information campaign. In time I began to realize that my job had become just a job and that my best efforts were being spent in my volunteer "career." The problem was, I still had to go to my job every day to earn a salary.*
>
> *The solution came in gaining clarity about how to use my best skills to make a living again. I quit my job and now work as a consultant and keynote speaker on issues relating to the aging population, bringing together my love of words, causes, and people in an independent but income-generating job.*

ॐ ॐ ॐ

That's the story of one individual who, without meaning to, found herself doing work she truly didn't like doing. We're not saying that you have to love all the aspects of your work. But if you don't like your job, it's going to affect your performance and how you feel about yourself. Many people share feelings of dissatisfaction and frustration in their jobs. If you are among them, if you feel that you're not doing your best work in your current situation, then what we're suggesting is that you gain clarity about your best achievements in order to move forward with understanding and control.

Best-Work Achievements, Not Jobs

Your qualities, strengths, and skills will pull you toward the work you do best. But you will find a way to do your best work for a living only if you take time to look back and sort out your values and preferences. Rather than thinking of the list of jobs you've had from past to present, try to think more broadly of your work experiences in terms of activities that used your skills in ways you preferred and that resulted in your best achievements—paid or unpaid.

So We Asked an Expert. Amy C. Fox, Accounting Analyst Recruiter, Kohler Co., says: "We can tell whether someone will be an exceptional employee by their personality, whether they're outgoing and straightforward. For example, we ask them what they liked and didn't like about former jobs. If they tell us they did data entry but didn't like it, we like that because we want them to be more analytical in this job."

The Point: Knowing your strengths and preferences offers an immediate advantage to employers as they envision putting you to work in their setting.

Preferences and Strengths

Your strengths will be a combination of your skills and preferences. Whatever your skills may be, you will have certain ones you prefer to use and certain ways you prefer to use them. Study the skills and achievements you've noted as most satisfying. Think about what your choices reveal about the ways you prefer to work.

· Do I like to work alone or with others?
· Do I like to plan ahead or dive into things?
· Do I like to be a leader or part of a team?

· What kind of values inspire me?
· Would I rather plant the garden and tend it, or harvest and preserve the things that have grown?
· Do I need to have the big picture in mind to get started, or do I get started first and let the picture develop?
· Does pressure unnerve me, or does it stimulate me to action?
· Are my antennae turned toward other people for direction, or do I like to determine for myself a way to work?

Consider how you've answered these questions. What do your responses reveal about how you prefer to work?

You Have a Big Future in Garbage!

Here is an exercise to help you get focused. Pretend you've just moved to a new community, and you need to get a job. The only job available is that of a garbage collector. You will take the job on one condition: you must have a guarantee that you can do your best work. The hiring committee is willing to consider one qualification you may add to the job description that will guarantee you'll like the job and do it well. (One rule: salary is not an issue.)

Complete this statement: I will accept the job of garbage collector under the condition that _____.

When we've used this exercise in our workshop, some of the conditions people describe are:

· I can work whatever hours I choose.
· I can determine the route.
· I can do it alone.
· I get to fix the truck.
· I can create policies for how people must wrap and leave their garbage.
· I get to learn about the city's overall goals and visions about garbage.
· I get to drive the truck.
· I get some helpers.

What qualification did you set as a condition for accepting the job as garbage collector? What insights can you gain from this exercise about yourself and the preferences you bring to your work? For some people, flexibility, autonomy, and independence are important. For others, knowing the big picture is key. Some must have hands-on, experiential jobs. Others need to understand and agree with guiding principles or philosophies. Some seek a structured situation in which it's clear what's expected. Whatever your skills, you will have preferences about how you want to use them.

As you begin to realize your work preferences more clearly, you'll understand more about your work history—why some jobs were better for you, some worse. Moreover, you can begin to let go of any sense of failure you may be harboring about past difficult work experiences by realizing that when you've worked most closely to your nature and within your preferences, you were working at your best.

▪ USING YOUR BEST-WORK QUALIFICATIONS TO GAIN FOCUS ▪

Take your three or four best-work qualifications—the skills and strengths evident in your preferred achievements. Now, which one do you like using best of all? We'll use ourselves as examples. Pat enjoys writing and speaking. Both are communication skills, but she prefers public speaking over writing. Patty is very good at detailed research and writing, but, given a choice, she'd rather be conducting research. What about you? What is your favorite best-work qualification?

Now let's explore your choice, using the following questions to stimulate your thinking.

1. What is your earliest memory of accomplishment using this strength?
2. How have you used this strength in each of your work settings, either paid or unpaid?
3. How are you currently using this strength in your life and career?
4. Think big. If you could use this special "gift" to make a lasting difference in the world, what would you do and how would you do it?

5. If you were president of your own company starting next Monday, how would you put your best strength to work?

Your chosen best-work qualification reveals a lot about you. You'll use what you find out to focus on the strengths you will bring to your best work.

"Accidental" Gifts We Acquire

Understanding that successful and powerful careers are built on identifying and developing our best and favorite skills, we can look clearly at both our past and our future. But we should realize that sometimes our development is accidental.

Careers are often shaped by life events and unforeseen opportunities, periods of family priorities (such as childbearing, child-rearing, and caregiving for ill or aging parents), and periods of personal upheaval. Life tends to happen even as we pursue our day jobs. Our skills can grow and flourish as a result of life events and eventually increase our career value.

Eugene, a young client of ours who is a natural innovator and has been a leader since earliest school days, found his college years rudely interrupted when his motor scooter slid on a rain-slick street beneath the tires of a truck, resulting in several broken bones and other injuries. A few years later, in reflecting back, he was able to see his six-month period of convalescence as a valuable time in his personal development. During those months, he learned a great deal about restoration of strength, about rehabilitation of both muscles and attitude. He had a chance to read outside his academic discipline, and he chose biographies and memoirs of those who inspired others by overcoming difficulties. His injuries fell into perspective as he learned about the hardships endured by others. He gained a new and critical outlook by taking the time to face his accident and to realize the fragility of life in the hands of fate. The perspectives he gained added depth to his skills and values and breadth to his goals.

Since his recovery, he has increased his reach in every sense. Through innovative projects, he has lived and worked in several countries; he has taken up sports requiring commitment and endurance; his next career phase, now in the planning, is not simply about work but about the desire to become an involved member of a community and to give to others.

He might not have done these things if not for his accident. The lesson we can learn from this young man is that we may not know what we will do next in our careers. But if we take the time to understand and appreciate our unique and sometimes accidental experiences, we will learn more about ourselves, how we will work, and the contributions we can make. Another lesson: don't wait to be hit by a truck in order to begin the introspection.

Natural Skills Keep Growing

As you think about how you would like to work in the future, consider your adult life. What periods of career interruption occurred? If you stayed home with children, served in the military, spent time unemployed, continued your education, or got technical or other training, what were the skills and strengths you acquired in these periods?

Go deeper now. What aspects stand out as personally successful? As a mother or father of young children, were you especially organized or creative? While in a military unit, did you help build team spirit? If unemployed, did you find a way to structure your life, take up a hobby, or initiate new opportunities? As you were taking courses, did you sharpen your time management skills or experience new levels of concentration and discipline? Did you support yourself or earn financial support through scholarships or awards? What do these experiences say about you and what you can and prefer to do?

Whether your career has been satisfying or frustrating, the chances are pretty good that the growth of your most natural skills has continued. What you do best and what you like best will find a use, either in your job or in other parts of your life. The challenge now is to create a career direction that will allow your best and favorite skills to drive your success.

Future Career Directions: Choice or Chance?

Consider two contrasting possibilities:

Possibility 1: Your career (your future working life) is going to go on whether you manage it or not. If you are passive, you will go in a variety of directions, meandering, picking up various skills and experiences, but not having an overall vision. If you were to draw a "career path" depicting random decisions with no career vision, it would look like this:

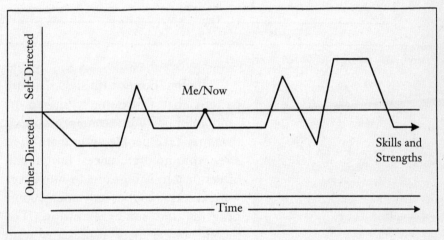

Career path with random pattern.

Possibility 2: You take control by planning for and seeking work that matches your strengths, and end up with a directed career, continuously gaining ground and demonstrating your best work. Your career path might look like this:

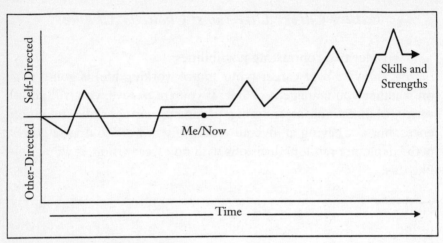

Career path, self-directed for best work.

So We Asked an Expert.
Teri Venker, Director of
Marketing and University
Relations, University of Wisconsin Colleges, states: "I
expect my employees to have
suggestions about their career
development as well as about
meeting organizational goals.
Someone who is growing on
the job is enthusiastic and
productive."
  The Point: Job commitment and professional self-
interest can, and should,
coexist in order to do your
best work.

The first career path shows a work pattern that is externally driven by random opportunities and promotions that may take people away from their strengths and preferences. Jumping at offers or job listings just to move forward creates random movement, some progress and some regression. The second career path represents what your best work will look like in the future if you develop a vision and take action to reach your goals. It will be ever-changing, with the ups and downs of taking risks, but it can be ever-improving—if you manage it well.

▪ BEWARE: JOB WITH A CAPE! ▪

A special warning is necessary here. Beware of the "job with a cape." Remember the fairy-tale heroes who come riding in on a white horse to rescue the heroines? Jobs with capes are those glamorous opportunities presented by others who promise to rescue us from our present situation.

The most seductive of these jobs are those that others tell us are "perfect" for us. Not only are we going to be rescued, but we feel flattered to be chosen and we naturally feel obliged to get on the horse. Thus a great salesman becomes a sales manager. A brilliant teacher becomes a curriculum director. A talented mechanic becomes a service station owner. An enthusiastic communicator becomes a direct-mail manager. All of these individuals are "rescued" from their strengths—just for the sake of galloping forward.

Jobs with capes typically lead us astray for three years, five years, ten years . . . before we realize we could have rescued ourselves if we wanted to move forward. The salesman could have found a company to reinspire him and offer a more profitable territory. The teacher might have become a corporate trainer. The mechanic could now be a hands-on instructor at a technical school. The communicator could be writing a book to help others rather than worrying over response rates on a spreadsheet.

We all know that it's important to progress in our careers, but it's equally important to fire up our best-work qualifications to propel us forward. It's critical to use the skills we most enjoy using. In the chapters to come, we will get specific about creating strategies based on your strengths and preferences. We'll offer suggestions and methods for acquiring information and using new tools to shape your career. The habit of analyzing your past work experience will continue to be central in directing your career. In fact, we think you'll come to appreciate and enjoy adding up your achievements. But do not leave this chapter until you can thoroughly complete the action steps we recommend.

So We Asked an Expert. Susan Tikalsky, President, Resource Strategies, Inc., notes: "I do inquire about personal things, such as 'What do you do with a spare Saturday afternoon? What are you reading these days? Who is the best boss you've ever worked for and why? What was your greatest accomplishment—and it definitely doesn't have to be work-related.' In fact, I prefer if it isn't."

The Point: What you do off the job shows the kind of person you are and the kind of employee you will be.

ACTION STEPS FOR GREATER CLARITY ABOUT YOUR SKILLS, PREFERENCES, AND STRENGTHS

1. Continue working on your history of best achievements and continue to analyze your work and identify strengths, skills, and preferences.
2. Continue to note and work on descriptions of your "best work" qualifications.
3. Imagine at least one fantasy project for your future that could use your strengths. Pretend you are in charge of all aspects of the project. Which roles will you personally take on to contribute your best work?
4. List the ways you have been sidetracked or misplaced in work projects or past jobs. List two or three potential "jobs with capes" that could, *in the future*, threaten to take you away from a self-directed approach to your career.
5. Add new thoughts to your notebook under "Gaining Clarity."

Using What You Know to Take Control of Your Career

Russell had decided to "take control" of his career. He had endured three consecutive phases of work that seemed to be taking him farther and farther away from anything he enjoyed. He began a process of clarification.

He thought about who he was and what values moved him. He began to consider the life stages he could predict in the near future—continued parenting, sending the kids to college, and eventually a comfortable empty nest. He had not yet fully explored his comfort level with risk, his appetite for change, or the parameters that he assumed kept him within certain boundaries. But Russell was starting to "get it." Big-time. He was starting to envision some ways he could move forward with self-determination.

Then a headhunter called. "I have a position open in Atlanta, but they need to fill it fast. Are you interested?" Russell answered, "Yes. I can fly down tomorrow." He got the job.

Sounds like a successful ending, right? Particularly for the headhunter, who received the usual commission for filling a corporate need fast. Russell, his wife, and two middle-school kids moved to Atlanta and were settled in within a month. Russell quit six months later. For the usual reason: it was work he could do, but work he didn't want to do.

What went wrong? Nobody was trying to hurt Russell's career. On the other hand, nobody was trying to help it either.

The process of sorting through our lives to reshape our careers can feel like being lost in a blizzard of new ideas, insights, and information. It's tempting to think that one phone call, one book, or one counselor holds the direction out of the storm. Sometimes we are too willing to rush in a new direction even when we know we're on a slick surface with little traction.

There's a lot of terrible advice out there. Over the years, we've become increasingly concerned about career-related advice offered by counselors in higher education, some of whom have never worked outside of their institutions. The focus, especially in business and professional schools, seems to be more on high placement rates than on providing meaningful guidance. This approach may get students a job, but it will not necessarily get them a satisfying career position.

Here's something to remember: before you start any course of action related to your career, make a firm commitment to retain control of the process and make decisions based on your own careful thinking and understanding of your needs and goals. You owe that commitment to yourself.

▪ CAREER "SHOULDS" WORTH QUESTIONING ▪

For every stage of work or career, there seems to be a list of "shoulds" that need to be recognized, then set aside. They include the classic plums—traditional thoughts about careers that are seldom, if ever, relevant to life on this planet at the start of the twenty-first century. Here are some examples.

· You *should* get a college degree (or an additional degree). Not always. Education is valuable in and of itself, but a formal degree is not always necessary for a career. Knowledge, skills, and credentials are available in a myriad of other learning settings, including excellent vocational schools. The real issue is finding out *what you need to learn for the life you want to live*. If you get a degree, it should be because you truly want to deepen or expand your knowledge, not because it will get you a job.
· You *should* know what you want to be. Few people do. Living and working with self-understanding will gradually reveal what you

want to be. Your vision will change numerous times throughout a lifetime.

· You *should* get a career position immediately out of college in your major field. You will. As long as you are learning and building skills that *matter to you* (and that's the key), any position will be a career position.

· You *should* be ready to go where the jobs are. Not so fast. Geographical location is of primary importance to most of us. Following a job to an undesirable location can make the work undesirable, too. Location decisions need to be made within the context of your whole life.

· You *should* be thankful you have a job at all and be satisfied with what you have. Don't buy it. This is a scary attitude, because the underlying message implies an "unworthiness." What happens to people who stay with what they have, feeling unworthy of anything better? (We think you know the answer to that.)

We believe that there are some wonderful career planning books available today. But we feel compelled to offer a few words of caution.

Some of the books want to take you too far inside yourself and can promote self-indulgence when they direct you to spend a good deal of time wishing or blissing over what you will be "when you grow up." You *are* grown-up, and you need to be serious about your life without being self-absorbed.

At the other end of the spectrum are the books that take you too far outside of yourself and give very specific and often ridiculous advice, such as sending out forty résumés a day, wearing a white (or sometimes blue) shirt, and putting on lipstick that's a bit darker than usual if you're over forty (and a woman, we presume). These books imply that a good, aggressive strategy and a few "tricks" are all you need to succeed and that beating others in the frantic race for a job is the goal.

We've met dozens of people who've made career decisions based on outdated or poor advice, people who have never developed the necessary sense of their own authority about how they want to work and whom they want to approach. Once you know who you are, it will be easy enough to figure out the color of your shirt and the shade of your lipstick.

▪ PITFALLS THAT GET IN THE WAY OF DOING YOUR BEST WORK ▪

There are also serious and life-consuming pitfalls when you go too far afield inside or outside of yourself. Consider the following possibilities.

- Those who buy the idea that the "image" of success *is* success often follow conventional paths, get seduced by a "job with a cape," and then find themselves glancing around the corporate meeting table years later still wondering how they should behave and what they should think or say next.
- Those who compete relentlessly to "get the job" may find, once they have it, that they're flushed and panting heavily from the race but actually wondering, "What exactly is this job?"
- People we know and love sometimes tell us (ever so respectfully, of course) that expecting our jobs and careers to be personally relevant is self-indulgent. These are often people who have become certified martyrs with miserable work lives. And they spend lots of time at work talking about their victimization.
- Other people state (rightfully at times) that making a career change can threaten their retirement benefits. This *is* an issue of parameters and risk, but it seems a shame to keep a lousy job and hope your life goes by really, really fast so you can retire comfortably.
- One fellow found an original approach. He talked his wife into having another baby, and now they have a very real reason for not rocking the career boat.
- New graduates, tired of flinching at family gatherings when relatives ask, "What are you going to do with your degree?" sometimes find graduate school to be a great escape. At least it keeps them from having to face the job market.

▪ GETTING BACK TO CENTER ▪

Most of the people we meet truly want to be successful by doing their best work. They want:

· To win a job legitimately because they are the best one for it
· To respect themselves and build a career carefully
· To enjoy their work and not wish their lives away
· To create career changes as their lives change
· To see how education works by working with their education

We've all seen the bumper sticker that says "Question Authority!" We particularly loved seeing it stuck to a bumper upside down. Get it? If you're going to question authority, turn every authority upside down. Don't go too far afield following the ideas of any expert out there. After all, in your life, who's more expert than you?

As we've said earlier, it's not easy learning to understand yourself and manage your work within the context of your life. It's difficult to let go of the old conventions, to stay on center. But it's extremely valuable. Once you've acquired the habit of managing your career, your efforts will become more and more automatic and your investment in Clarity, Strategy, and Action will pay lifetime dividends. In two, five, thirteen years, you won't even remember a time when you didn't know how to manage your career.

▪ IT'S IMPORTANT TO KNOW YOUR LIMITS AND TO KNOW WHEN TO TEST THEM ▪

Getting beyond the "shoulds" and the pitfalls is necessary. But it's complicated.

The direction we can or will take is defined by our boundaries or parameters. Parameters are neither good nor bad in themselves, but there are two points to keep in mind: *you* should determine your parameters, and you should do so *for good reasons*.

Sometimes we allow parameters to exist and assume great importance without good reasons. Several of our clients over the years have claimed "home ownership" as a parameter that limits their ability to leave a dissatisfying job. The payments, after all, must be made. In several cases, however, clients came to realize that selling the house not only was a possibility but would create new financial, geographic, lifestyle, and career opportunities by allowing new freedoms to flow. In these cases, home ownership was a parameter worth reexploring.

Sometimes we aren't even aware of the parameters we've set; they simply seem like unchangeable life conditions. A friend in Washington was convinced at midlife that she needed to stay in Yakima, where her grown children lived, to be near her grandchildren and to be available as needed. Her job at that time, as a hairdresser in a nursing home, had begun to depress her. She described hearing elderly clients, day after day, speak mostly of regrets about their lives— "I wish I would have; I'm so sorry that I didn't; if I had it to do over again . . ." They all spoke of risks not taken, dreams unfulfilled. Their message began to sink in, and the hairdresser began to imagine taking a risk and starting a new life. Her decision was made the day she overheard one of her grown children ask another, "Who's taking Mom this weekend?" She was shocked. She was only forty-seven. She had stayed in Yakima out of obligation to her family. She realized, however, that they felt burdened by her. So she sold her house, bought a comfortable condo in Seattle, and quickly found work to support a new lifestyle. The punch line: her kids now call to schedule their turns for visits. By pushing aside the perceived parameter, she was able to broaden the vista not only for herself but for those she loves as well. She recently told us with a mischievous grin, "I don't see the kids too often. I really have a lot going on in my new life."

Parameters aren't always negotiable, nor should they be overthrown without careful thought. A spouse's employment, health-related issues, and caregiving responsibilities, for example, can be nonnegotiable. Strong preferences can become genuine parameters, such as unwillingness to leave a geographic area, choosing to keep children in a particular school, or assuming financial responsibilities.

To create a framework for possible new directions, list the factors in your life that seem to form boundaries or parameters that either limit or expand your vision.

PARAMETERS	NEGOTIABLE	NONNEGOTIABLE
	(I Need to question this.)	(I choose to honor this.)

Reflect on these parameters and how they will affect the career opportunities you might pursue and how they define your values.

▪ RISK-TAKING: A HIGHLY PERSONAL MATTER ▪

As you consider future directions, realize that the ability to take risks or the desire to avoid them is also a highly individual characteristic. Again, neither taking nor avoiding risks is in itself good or bad. There are people who suffer great stress when they have to take a risk. Interestingly, there are also people who suffer great stress when their world feels too safe and predictable. Such people can become depressed, understimulated, and unproductive as a result.

Part of your history of successful achievement has to do with how you've managed risk. Whatever your skill level in risk management, you will be able to avoid undue anxiety during a period of career exploration by:

- Creating a structured, self-determined plan to explore career change, rather than engaging in a random, panicky approach
- Setting aside specific and regular time to work on job and career issues
- Finding agreement with a spouse, partner, or roommate about needs and resources such as space, time, and financial flexibility
- Arranging a "checkpoint" relationship with a colleague to measure progress and set next-step goals
- Framing all the unknowns during this time as a period of growth and necessary adventure—and learning to enjoy it

Go back to your Lifeline and Me/Now point. As you consider the future, picture yourself in a wilderness area facing one of those hiking trail markers that show you where you are on the path you've taken so far. Imagine the map shows a six-mile loop and that it represents a potential direction your career might take.

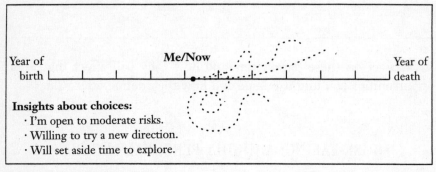

Year of
birth   Me/Now   Year of
                                                                                   death

Insights about choices:
· I'm open to moderate risks.
· Willing to try a new direction.
· Will set aside time to explore.

Lifeline: Ah, wilderness!

Do you take this loop? What are the alternatives? How many other loops exist? How steep or challenging might this trail be compared with others depicted on the map? How scenic? How dangerous? What is the weather? The condition of the trail?

This analogy is apt. Wherever you are, there are any number of ways to move forward. The six-mile career loop may be the one you will eventually take, but you may want to consider the alternative one-mile trek as a way to get started.

Focus on the Me/Now for a moment. How fresh are you feeling? Are your boots right for the trail? What supplies are you carrying? Is there a path you have in mind that isn't shown on the map? In other words, if there are career directions

So We Asked an Expert: Keith Kluender, Associate Chair, Department of Psychology, University of Wisconsin-Madison, says: "New career directions can sometimes be found close to where you already are. I've been fortunate to find continuing challenges but only by taking charge and initiating new directions enthusiastically."

The Point: Doing your best changes as skills and abilities increase. It's up to you to identify the next trail and take it.

or opportunities that have nothing to do with the work you've done in the past or the trail you think you'll eventually take, this might be the time to explore them. The appeal of new explorations is often connected to skills, values, and a sense of potential we intuitively believe we have. Can you risk it? Could you forge a new trail if necessary?

As you have begun to select your best-work qualifications, you have been identifying the very resources that will help you explore new directions. The trek can be within the scope of your experience or in new areas of interest. The important thing now is to take a few steps. Don't just stand there looking at the map.

▪ FIGURING OUT WHERE YOU WANT TO GO ▪

Think about the words you might use in "headlines" you would choose if you were to run an advertisement for yourself: strong communicator, outstanding human relations skills, specific technical knowledge or skills, effective resource management, good administrator, strong decision-maker, detail-focused perfectionist, innovator, visionary. Once you define your marketable skills, you will be able to set out on trails leading to whatever goals matter most to you:

- · Increased income
- · Further skill development
- · Work with deep, personal meaning
- · A brand-new experience
- · Unknown territory
- · Balance and restoration through familiar work

Or, as one friend put it, just more time for fly fishing!

It's hard to decide for ourselves which trails to explore. In an age in which even the road less taken seems crowded with followers, it's all too easy to keep watching where others have gone or are going. But if you start with an understanding of your best-work qualifications and a simple statement of even a small goal, the trail will begin to reveal itself. Why does this happen? Because the clearer you are about yourself, the clearer you will be about the direction that makes the most sense for you.

▪ TAKING CONTROL OF YOUR CAREER ▪

We believe that taking control of your career is comparable to an intense, rigorous journey in the wilderness. It's full of discovery and exercising muscles you don't often use. Stepping ahead boldly and with new clarity can be jarring at first when we realize how removed we have become from understanding ourselves. But movement is better than being stuck.

How much time and energy have we spent trying to compensate for a miserable job? How long have we been licking our wounds from being fired or feeling marginalized? How often have we stepped on our colleagues' hands while clumsily scrambling up a ladder? These are harder occupations than moving forward with diligent integrity. As you understand more about who you are and how you want to work, your career path will be a beautiful trail that you alone determine. You'll become exhilarated by your increased strength and the clear air you are breathing.

Bear with the metaphor just a little longer. You don't start by leaping to the trail's end. Instead, you select a trailhead and figure out the first few steps. Be warned: you'll find countless reasons and excuses for not starting out.

Why don't people take those steps? Here are some standard excuses. But in making these excuses, the people are staying stuck, probably frustrated. Meanwhile, that's not time going by—it's their lives.

THOSE WHO ARE:	FREQUENTLY SAY:
Employed	I have more to do than is humanly possible already.
Unemployed	I don't have time to sit and plan. I have pavements to pound, classified ads to fit into, fifty résumés a day to send out!
Underemployed	Every day is a struggle. It's all I can do just to get by.
Starting out	Nobody starts with the ideal job. I'll just do this for a few years.
Winding down	Just two more years and I'm outta here.

You don't have to feel this way. Here are some alternative ways to think about the possibilities.

IF YOU ARE:	FOCUS ON:
Employed	Developing my best work on my next project in my current job
Unemployed	Adding my best work to day-to-day challenges
Underemployed	Using my best work outside of work
Starting out	Seeking advice and opportunity for offering my best work
Winding down	Exploring new applications for my best work

Now let's look at some examples of how people start down the trail to the best work of their lives.

Reggie: Employed and Not Ready to Leave His Job

Reggie, associate director of a large trade association, was skilled at developing new programs. He was not ready to leave his job. He loved innovation and was great at human relations but felt hampered by the constant bottom-line focus of his boss. "More money!" was the continuous command from above. Reggie felt dead in the water from continuing to wring profits from existing programs, taking little risk on anything new, and maintaining routine contact with coworkers.

He decided to revitalize his best-work qualifications by talking to suppliers, calculating the risk of several new initiatives, and projecting possible outcomes. Because the success of a new venture would be based on Reggie's best-work skills—innovation, planning, and strong relationship building—he came alive as the possibilities evolved. He proposed a new program to his boss, who was willing to take a risk. Reggie had done the calculations and he explained the risk thoroughly. His boss was also motivated by Reggie's enthusiasm. Within a year, Reggie had created an increased revenue stream of 15 percent with this successful new venture. The boss was happy, the money was flowing, and, best of all, Reggie's name was all over this success. People inside his work setting, his suppliers, and peers within his professional network now see who Reggie is more clearly because he demonstrated his best work as he built success for his organization. Reggie revitalized his job, but more important, he revitalized himself and continues to recognize further opportunity based on his success.

Debra: Unemployed but More Engaged in Her Best Work Than Ever Before

Debra lost her job because, as a devoted single parent, she was frequently absent from work or taking time away to participate in her children's activities. Her workplace, while a pleasant environment, was not flexible enough for her needs. It was clear that her best-work skills—systems analysis, detail focus, and strong commitment—were more successfully evident in her thriving children's lives than in her job performance. She signed on with a temporary agency to earn a minimal income, pared away all but the essentials in her budget, and began her real work—becoming involved in the local issues of her children's school district. Although she had no college degree and lived on very little income, she became a critical resource in improving the schools in her district through a growing understanding of the issues, her ability to organize others, and her knowledge (from her professional experience) of how to make systems work better.

When we last spoke with her, she had begun exploring two possible future directions: lobbying and running for a local public office. Meanwhile, she said, the years with her children are being greatly enriched by their understanding of who she really is as she works to better their school environment.

Lydia: Underemployed and Her Spirit Flagging

Lydia, a Harvard-educated lawyer, found herself bored and unsatisfied in her corporate firm. Her intellect was fully engaged in her career, but her best-work qualifications—creativity, passion, and an extraordinary ability to captivate people with her humor and warmth—were seriously underutilized. In addition, she had a secret yearning to write film reviews. She loved movies and often found herself in long conversations with friends analyzing films they had seen. She felt unable to leave her job, but she decided to take a chance and wrote several movie reviews. Her entertaining articles were published in small, local newspapers. She gained a sense of herself that allowed her creativity to flow further, and, ultimately, she added an amazing achievement to her life. Passionate about women's issues, Lydia drew on her best-work skills and created a film series for a local battered women's shelter. Each week she would select and show a violence-related movie to the women in residence. With the help of the staff counselors, she would then lead a discussion about the film, relating it to the issues of real violence the women had experienced. Using her best skills helped Lydia remember what it feels like to be excited about work.

Elle: Starting Out but Looking for More

Elle, a new college graduate with an English degree, took a position at a small fine arts college as the work/study coordinator. The pay was terrible, but the job used some of her best skills: strong human relations, writing and speaking, and information management. It was apparent that pay increases were doomed to be minimal and that there was little chance for promotion because the staff remained firmly in place year after year. Elle decided that there could be more career value in expanding the use of her best-work qualifications. She volunteered for committees related to staff issues. In a short time, she was elected as chair of the staff council. During her three-year, entry-level work experience, Elle developed her job skills and added new ones by using her natural talent as an advocate for others. Her résumé and her sense of value were significantly enriched by the skills she chose to offer in addition to those her job officially required. The opportunities had been close at hand. The new trail was interwoven with the one she was already following.

Paul: Winding Down—but He's Also Revving Up!

Paul was two years from retirement. He'd worked in middle management, for what felt like forever, and he was counting the months until he could get out. Increasingly, though, he wondered if his retirement funds would be enough to live on. His wife, Karen, worked part-time and had no intention of retiring yet. Karen had also been sending not-so-subtle signals about hoping Paul would have enough to do after retirement and warning him not to become a couch potato. Paul began to think about his career. He vaguely remembered times he'd been truly stimulated and felt useful. While looking back, his view toward the future became clear. He figured a few things out. Paul's best career achievements had been tied to project management. His best projects lasted an average of one to three years before he grew bored. The projects had consisted of studying and researching a problem, constructing several possible plans, leading others in a review of facts for decision-making, and finally selecting one strategic plan. He realized how much he'd enjoyed the hands-on part of starting a new program, how he liked to step back, watch it grow, and manage it with a light hand. And he liked tracking reports showing results that would help in the next planning cycle.

A wave of new clarity hit him like the proverbial ton of bricks. No wonder Paul loved the gardening projects he'd taken on in his community in recent years. Every phase drew on his best skills—research, planning, and teamwork. Tilling the soil, planting the seeds, overseeing the growth, harvesting the crops, and refining the design: these were his specialties. With two years remaining until his retirement, Paul realized that he could change his career completely and still continue to do his best work. It didn't take long for him to explore gardening associations near and far, to network on the "greenhouse circuit," to start researching public and private parks. He's not there yet, but Paul is on his way to a retirement career.

The Lessons

In each of these examples, individuals found opportunity wherever they were, whatever their employment status. They found opportunity by starting with a recognition of who they are and how their best and favorite skills can be put to work in new ways. In subsequent chapters we'll discuss how such people strategically move forward to explore even greater opportunity. For now, though, think about your best-work qualifications and how you can move at least a few steps from where you are, to show others and to remind yourself of the value you uniquely offer.

▪ FINDING BALANCE IN YOUR LIFE ▪

Personal balance is one of the most important but elusive goals in the current work world. We yearn for an ideal way to work that will allow us to be fully human, to have a life that is creative, personally fulfilling, a life that is productive yet socially relevant and responsible. Balance can best be created by understanding how our needs and our activities are interconnected.

The LifeCircle is a visual symbol for considering balance in our lives. We will refer to this diagram as a construct for considering work in its widest perspective. The LifeCircle will also help you broaden your thinking about how your best work might fit into the world.

Here's the LifeCircle:

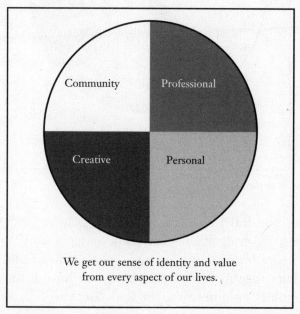

We get our sense of identity and value
from every aspect of our lives.

LifeCircle: Symbol of the activities of our lives.

Let's assume that your life falls into perfect order in these four quadrants. You spend your time and energy equally on all priorities. Not only would your life be balanced, but your identity would be drawn from complementary activities. Good works in the community, strong personal relationships, and creative interests would all contribute to a healthy and productive work life. It's an ideal worth striving for.

But if you're like most of us, your diagram looks more like this:

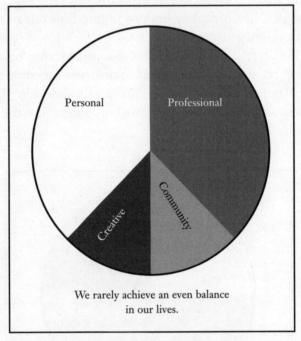

LifeCircle: Symbol of the activities of our lives.

There is no ideal LifeCircle. It is used as a way to expand your thinking and to understand that achievements and opportunities abound in many settings. For example, people may fulfill their need for community identity and personal relationships in the workplace, while community volunteers might find potential for greater career development outside traditional work settings.

Here's how it works for Reggie, Elle, Debra, Paul, and Lydia:

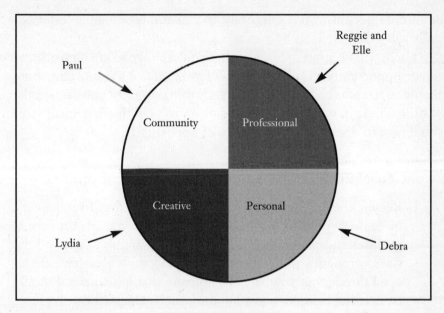

LifeCircle: Opportunity exists in every aspect of our lives.

As we continue to work with clients like Lydia, Reggie, Debra, Elle, and Paul, we encourage them to look at all the quadrants of their lives and to start imagining their exploration for opportunities in all four areas. We also remind them that by looking at their lives from four different perspectives they will begin to remember past achievements from settings outside of their professional role.

Consider your LifeCircle. Are you engaged in all aspects of your life or what your life could be? Think about the kind of balance you'd like to achieve. What goals could you achieve in each area by doing your best work? You have strengths and skills, values and accomplishments, in all areas of your life. And if you are feeling lopsided, this is the time to set some goals for the future. Want more balance? Step away from your professional identity. Pick another quadrant. Create a goal, strive for it, achieve it, and *voilà!*—you will have stronger qualifications for the workplace. Meet with community members and you'll grow a new network. Run in a charity marathon and you will have achieved new levels of discipline and endurance. Read a good novel and your imagination will be fired up for those tough problems at work. Spend time really listening to your spouse or another person who is important to you and your human relations skills will grow.

There will be strategic approaches you can take to create work and career opportunity in all the areas of your life. It's important, now, simply to stretch the boundaries of your thinking until you can see the full LifeCircle in which you live and begin to plan the first small steps you'll take to discover an abundance of opportunity.

ACTION STEPS TO TAKE CONTROL OF YOUR CAREER

1. Review the Lifelines you've sketched in the first five chapters. Note the key events that have influenced who you are, the natural qualities and patterns of behavior that distinguish you, and the skills, strengths, preferences, values, and goals that have developed throughout your life. The picture that has emerged should be rich and complex and an unmistakable self-portrait.
2. Continue to refine two to four best-work qualifications you would most like to use in the future.
3. Identify the immediate steps you can take to apply your best-work qualifications right now, whether you are employed, unemployed, underemployed, just starting out, or finally winding down.
4. Study the LifeCircle and begin to construct one for yourself to expand your sense of opportunity as we begin to move toward strategic planning.

Part II

STRATEGY

Chapters 6–10 will help you build strategies to go after the best work of your life. With a new sense of clarity you'll be able to present your achievements in a way that will create expanded opportunity. The skills, values, and preferences that characterize your accomplishments will come together with the parameters, goals, and choices you determine for the way you want to work in the future.

A new perspective about your work will enable you to speak clearly with personal authority about your qualifications. As that happens, you'll begin to identify people to seek out to expand your knowledge and broaden your view. Understanding the scope of opportunity will lead you to valuable information and help to define your strategy.

Strategic thinking and planning are lifelong activities. Once you've learned how to move forward from the present to a well-planned future, you'll gain the confidence to continue moving toward your goals. The tools and tactics we offer in these chapters will help you initiate a strategy to do your best work. You'll know it when you find it. It will be the work you can't wait to do.

six

The Ah-ha Résumé

Kim-Lee had two goals. To get a job and to get it in Chicago. She had a fresh diploma from a major university (B.S. in biology) and a history of employment that included pizza waitress, office worker, and assorted summer jobs. She labored over her résumé and, after a lot of squishing and squeezing, ended up with a tight, one-page summary of her jobs in reverse chronological order. Her name, address, phone number, and brand-new degree were listed at the top. She took the disk with her résumé to a photocopy shop and had thirty copies laser-printed. Next, she scoured the classified ads in the weekend *Chicago Tribune* and picked out thirty—everything and anything. Kim-Lee composed a short, general cover letter ("To whom it may concern") and for under one hundred dollars (printing, stationery, envelopes, postage) sent the résumés off. Then she waited.

Several companies sent generic postcards acknowledging receipt of her résumé. Five sent letters promising to schedule an interview. Three actually called. All wanted her to come to Chicago (on different days) to meet in person. Kim-Lee began a flurry of round trips (driving three hundred miles each time) for the interviews. Two were large group interviews; one was face-to-face with a company representative. Two wanted to do follow-up interviews (two more round trips). In the end, Kim-Lee had two job offers, both entry-level, both at minimum wage, both on the retail floor.

She had achieved her goal—a job offer in Chicago. Her strategy worked—flood the universe with one-page résumés. However, Kim-Lee couldn't afford to accept such low-paying jobs, didn't want to work in retail, and was already several hundred dollars in the hole just from travel, printing, and postage expenses. The companies offering the jobs were offering them to just about anyone who applied. Kim-Lee had simply been caught in the big net they were casting to fill numerous new retail positions. You, too, can do that. But don't!

▪ RÉSUMÉ MYTHS, TRICKS, AND FEARS ▪

It continues to shock us that no matter how much clarity people get about how marketable they are because of who they are, they still freeze up and fall back on myths, tricks, and fears when it comes to their résumés.

The *myths* tell us that résumés:

· Must fit on one page
· Should list every job you've ever had
· Should include only paid employment
· Should be sent by the carload
· Will be carefully read by the receivers
· Will make sense to others

The *tricks* in résumé lore tell us to:

· Make it look "creative" with cute graphics
· Fold it in an odd way to make it (literally) stick out in a pile
· Use a special-color paper
· Use an obscure professional dialect with no pronouns

Our résumé *fears* cause us to:

· Exaggerate accomplishments, titles, and responsibilities
· Hide our age

· Cover up gaps in work history
· Worry about formal educational credentials

Today it's possible to find hundreds of formats for the "perfect" résumé. Just get on the Internet or go to a library or bookstore and check out the various examples available. You'll find that there are résumés tailored for special careers and even structured résumé formats using keywords that employers can scan with computer software.

No matter what form your résumé takes, it's the content that will determine the quality of opportunities it creates by showing the value you have to offer. The strategy—whom you will offer it to and how you will do that—will be determined by the content you *choose* to include. For now, though, the focus is on how to identify your best-work achievements and put them on paper in a way that will indicate the best work you will do in the future.

Most people feel painfully intimidated about résumés. Many believe there is a secret formula for a good résumé, and they apologize for never having discovered it. We hear comments like "My résumé is really out of date, is in bad shape, looks terrible, is pretty hard to figure out." Or "I have a better one on a disk somewhere—or in a drawer." We're reminded of the guy driving the clunker with a bumper sticker that says "My other car is a Mercedes." Most of us hope that a perfect résumé, once created, will land us a perfect job.

▪ THE AH-HA RÉSUMÉ ▪

What if we told you that there is a winning résumé format—one that will put your work into a meaningful perspective and help shape your future work life? One résumé has such power. We call it the Ah-ha résumé.

This is the mother of all résumés. Once you've done the work to create your Ah-ha résumé, you'll be able to fashion a variety of versions to use when particular formats are requested or required. The Ah-ha résumé will also:

· Help prepare you for interviews
· Become a script to use for interviews

· Provide a bank in which you deposit your accomplishments once you've added them up
· Allow you to review your life work and create meaningful and strategic direction
· Become the basis from which you can quickly create tailored résumés as you identify specific opportunities

Nothing cuts through the confusion of a "stuck" career like the Ah-ha résumé. Nothing helps clarify direction for those beginning a career like the Ah-ha résumé. Nothing helps a person go after a promotion or a new project in a current work setting like the Ah-ha résumé. Why? Because of the *Ah-ha*.

> **So We Asked an Expert.** Susan Tikalsky, President, Resource Strategies, Inc., says: "A skill-based résumé shows me that the person has more experience and they understand themselves better. They can articulate their value. I don't look at chronological ones anymore."
> **The Point:** Employers want to see right away how your abilities can add value to their organization. Show them as directly as possible.

The Ah-ha résumé does not have some special format or any other gimmick like that. It's about who you are and what you have to offer. The Ah-ha comes as you determine the stories the résumé will tell. Stories of the best achievements in your life so far. Stories from paid employment and other settings that describe the challenges you faced, the steps you took to meet those challenges, and the final, concrete results of your achievements. The Ah-ha occurs when you look at your résumé and say, "Now, this is me!" (and not somebody I'm trying to make people think I am).

Find Yourself in Your Best Achievements

We were working with a client not long ago in what was becoming an increasingly clumsy attempt to help him. Julio had called us because he was stuck in a longtime sales-related position with a company that was in trouble in an industry that was struggling. Not a pretty picture. Not only did Julio want out of his situation, he wanted way out. "I'll move somewhere—anywhere!" he said, convinced by now that only a catapult approach could spring him from his misery.

His frustration was palpable. We weren't sure where to start. Julio didn't have much clarity, he had no strategy, and we felt that no information would be helpful until we found a way to focus. We talked about work-related values. We talked about possible new locations. Every conversation came unanchored—until we decided to get Julio to focus on his résumé. We figured an Ah-ha moment couldn't hurt.

Julio brought his old résumé to our next meeting. It was well organized but dull and impersonal. He mumbled a few apologies. As we looked over the list of Julio's old jobs and work history, we asked him to think of some "stories" of the best projects he'd done in these settings. We told him to forget the dates, titles, companies, and job duties listed on the old résumé and simply to remember the work experiences, describing aloud when and how he'd done his best work.

Julio blinked and leaned forward on the table between us. His dark eyes flashed with interest. "Wow. I was just remembering the time I was sent to Texas to try to reorganize a project because the office down there was in trouble."

As Julio described the challenges he'd faced, we took notes. As he remembered all the hard things he'd had to do, we wrote them down in a brief list. He was really enjoying the story and so were we. When he stopped, we pressed. "Tell us about the results of that project." He looked blank. "Oh, I guess it turned out okay," he said. "Not good enough," we responded. Then we forced Julio to think about the number of people he had affected, whether time or money was saved, how many customers were better served as a result. And, of course, there were many real results. He had just never bothered to add them up.

Julio's story revealed not only one solid résumé item but a lot about his characteristics—his leadership, ability to organize, fearless approach to problem-solving, concern with cutting costs, commitment to the success of others in his company. The way he told the story revealed his enthusiasm and the pride that comes from remembering your best moments. This is the stuff that powerful résumés are made of.

As Julio continued to develop his résumé, he identified his skills and began to see them in a different light. Perhaps they could be transferable to other companies or industries. He gained insight about his values and the goals that motivate him. He also realized that moving to another location could be a preference, not a necessity.

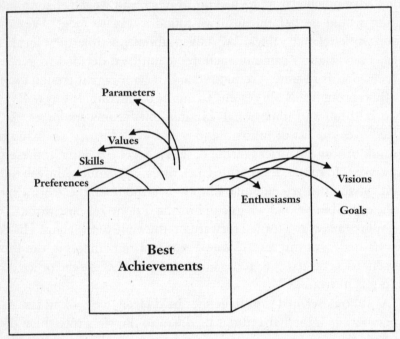

What you have to offer and what you are all about can be found by examining the "box" containing your best achievements.

As Julio continues to consider other achievements from his past, he'll be able to form at least a preliminary objective: to use his best strengths with enthusiasm to solve the challenges of potential employers. He will see his strongest qualifications clearly. In addition to realizing that his best work comes from being well organized, motivating others, maintaining deadlines, and delivering cost-saving results, Julio is becoming aware of the uniqueness of his character. He is loyal, disciplined, and courageous. These discoveries help him tailor his qualifications and envision potential challenges. As he searches through his past selecting his best achievements, a self-portrait will come into focus. "Ah-ha! This is me."

Sometimes when people become involved in reviewing their past successes, achievements outside the workplace come to mind. Julio, for example, mentioned that he had run eight marathons in recent years (commitment, discipline, endurance). He had helped a friend start a small business (organization, team management for the success of others). And he'd been a United Way volunteer (dedication and compassion). Key qualifications were becoming more evident. As Julio progressed in his career planning, he looked for companies and organizations that were in need of the specific strengths he had to offer and, in return, offered a match for his nature, values, and preferences.

Think back to Kim-Lee's Chicago résumé blitz. Remember that she'd used a reverse chronological format listing her jobs and noting her shiny, new degree. Her résumé, though neatly organized, told nothing of who she was. The companies that received it knew only what she told them: limited work experience, young graduate. They had every reason in the world to offer her only an entry-level job. Kim-Lee had given them no evidence of her special qualifications, achievements, or patterns in her life that would reveal all she had to offer.

Traditional résumé.

Kim-Lee Elliott
4291 Lambert Street
Madison, Wisconsin 53700
(608) 971-2021

Education:

University of Wisconsin–Madison, B.S. Biology, 1987

Work Experience:

1987–86
Manager, gift shop, University of Wisconsin Memorial Union. Part-time work in retail setting at university gift shop managing staff, sales and inventory.

1986 (July and August)
Summer job as waitress at Pizza House, Baraboo, Wisconsin. Responsibilities included opening and closing restaurant, waiting on customers, changing menu for daily specials and supplying wait-stations after each shift.

1986–85
Clerical worker for department of Biology, University of Wisconsin–Madison. Responsibilities included assisting professors on research projects, maintaining records and helping with grant writing.

1985–84 (Summers)
Summer staff position at Camp Wonewoc, Wonewoc, Wisconsin. Position required overseeing the start and end activities for each camp session, helping with other activities and coaching the swim team.

1985–84
Intern in State Legislature for Representative Joseph Alameda. General office duties. Assisted with special events. Answered constituents' calls and letters.

1985–84
Resident Adviser in women's dormitory, Chadbourne Hall, University of Wisconsin–Madison. Duties included holding orientation sessions for residents and being available 20 hours each week for meetings and projects.

Awards and Honors

Maintained 3.5 overall grade point average throughout college.
Student Government Leadership Award, University of Wisconsin–Madison, 1987.
Wonewoc Counselor of the Year, Camp Wonewoc, Wisconsin, 1985.
National Honors Society, Madison West High School, 1983–1984.

As Kim-Lee began to work with the Ah-ha Résumé format, she recognized patterns of leadership from extracurricular activities in high school and college. She realized that research and writing had been a part of every project she'd enjoyed. She saw, in her past, that she had managed a number of priorities simultaneously—part-time work and organizing a campus-wide project while maintaining a 3.5 grade point average in college. It occurred to her that "managing multiple priorities" might be worth mentioning on her résumé. She thought wistfully about the Chicago companies. "If only they had seen my real talents." If only she had told them!

Ah-ha résumé.

Kim-Lee Elliott
4291 Lambert Street
Madison, Wisconsin 53700
(608) 971-2021

Objective: Seeking opportunity to apply strong research and project management skills in collaborative setting in science-related corporation or organization.

Qualifications: Project leadership through effective management of multiple priorities. Disciplined research writing skills. Excellent human relations based on collaboration and team building.

Achievements:

Project Leadership

University of Wisconsin–Madison Campus Project. I coordinated a campus cross-peer mentoring program involving collaboration between student government and student dormitory council officers. I created a nine-month timeline, oversaw committee formation and task assignments for 42 student leaders. We averaged twice-weekly meetings and regular written communication for project progress. Outcomes included peer teams for cross-discipline quality improvement in student housing and related issues. In addition, we created leadership continuity planning. Pilot project resulted in measurable housing program improvements through special meetings and events involving over 800 students and faculty advisers. I received Student Government Leadership Award at project completion.

Research and Writing

As clerical staff in University of Wisconsin Biology Department I became research assistant to three professors seeking grants. I provided bimonthly list of new grant sources, reviewed criteria and researched pertinent data for proposal completion. I analyzed previous records to support proposals. Twelve grants, totaling $3.2 million, resulted from our collaborations.

As intern for Wisconsin State Representative Joseph Alameda I reviewed and analyzed key issues in relation to constituents' requests for information. I provided accurate written responses to over 200 callers and responded to 20–30 verbal requests weekly. I briefed legislative staff at weekly team meetings in regard to constituents' priority interests.

Human Relations

As manager of retail shop in University of Wisconsin Memorial Union which serves over 10,000 faculty, staff and students daily, I coordinated workers' schedules and job duties with attention to their academic needs in flexible planning. I oversaw vendor relations and managed inventory adjustments weekly. Our shop received citations for excellence from the Union Director three times in twelve months.

Page 2

As Resident Adviser for Chadbourne Hall Dormitory I was directly responsible for 138 students in residence. Duties included planning and conducting orientation sessions at each semester's start, weekly floor meetings with all residents and special events planning. In addition, I coordinated health and counseling services as needed, and met with other Resident Advisers on a monthly basis to continuously improve systems and services.

As camp counselor at Camp Wonewoc, Wisconsin, I helped establish pre-season planning events with staff for team building. Established arrival and departure procedures with individual focus on welcoming new campers. I assumed flexible assignments ranging from administrative duties to swim team coaching. We served 341 campers and welcomed over 500 parents to special events. Helped with retention planning resulting in 82% return of staff the following year.

Employment and Related Experience:
1987–86
Manager, Memorial Union Gift Shop, University of Wisconsin–Madison.
Campus Coordinator, Student Government Campus Mentoring Project.

1986–85
Research Assistant, Department of Biology, University of Wisconsin–Madison.
Legislative Intern, Representative Joseph Alameda, State Capitol, Madison, Wisconsin.
Waitress, Pizza House Restaurant, Baraboo, Wisconsin.

1985–84
Camp Counselor, Camp Wonewoc, Wonewoc, Wisconsin.
Resident Adviser, Chadbourne Hall, University of Wisconsin–Madison.

1984–80
Volunteer child care worker, Summer Streets Recreation Program, Madison, Wisconsin.
After-school child care provider throughout high school for local families.

Education and Training:
B.S. in Biology, University of Wisconsin–Madison, 1987 (3.5 overall grade point average). Completion of computer software applications courses including PageMaker, Excel. Power Point
Emergency Medical Training Certificate, 1984.
Annual Student Leadership Seminars at Big Ten Campus Conferences, 1984–87.

Awards and Honors:
Student Government Leadership Award, University of Wisconsin–Madison, 1987.
Dean's List, University of Wisconsin–Madison, 1986–87.
Counselor of the Year Award, Camp Wonewoc, Wisconsin, 1985.
National Honors Society, Madison West High School, 1983–84.

References furnished on request.

During the next few years, Kim-Lee refined her résumé and her job search strategy by matching her best qualifications with companies in need of them. She built a powerful start-up career as a research assistant in a pharmaceutical company, and later as a project director at the city's natural history museum. Eventually, she became a rising young star in the museum's administration, researching, writing, and winning grants for the organization. Her skills and experiences were continually enriched. She was also able to maintain clarity, refashioning her strategy as her best work increased in value.

Building the Perfect Résumé

In later chapters we'll focus on strategies for finding companies and job opportunities that will allow you to do the best work of your life. You may end up using various résumé formats to suit specific companies. But first, you need to create an Ah-ha résumé of your own to capture in words the marketplace value you offer. Don't think just yet about what's out there somewhere ahead of you. Think instead about what's in your past.

▪ THE AH-HA RÉSUMÉ: ELEMENTS IN ORDER OF APPEARANCE ▪

Working with the discoveries from the clarity exercises, let's lay the foundation for your Ah-ah résumé.

1. Objective: Brief statement of the goal you have in mind

The objective statement connects your desire to offer your best skills to the place they are most needed. It will be general at first and become more specific as you focus on particular organizations or companies.

Example (general): "Seeking opportunity to apply proven human relations and communications skills to increase organization's effectiveness."

Example (more focused): "Seeking opportunity to apply proven human relations and communications skills in publishing setting for increased productivity and profit."

Notice that your objective should be about both your qualifications and the needs of your prospective employers, clearly matching what you have to offer and what they want.

2. Qualifications: The unique "gifts" you have and choose to offer

You will create two to four "headlines" (as we discussed in Chapter 5), terms that powerfully summarize the qualities, strengths, and skills evident in your history of achievements. You'll list your strongest and favorite skill first, followed by the others. (If there is an area of skill or expertise in your work history you no longer enjoy using, omit it. This is your résumé, not your obituary!) Qualifications should be straightforward and appealing and should indicate the personal characteristics that distinguish how you work. A salesman we know chose "Legendary Customer Relations" rather than merely "strong" ones. He wanted the swagger of his success to show, and it was appropriate in his field.

To help you understand what we're doing here, we'll look at a few examples.

Let's say you've listed "strong leadership" as a qualification. Can you describe further your personal version of leadership? What does strong leadership mean to you? Is it any of the following?

· Strong collaborative leadership
· Leadership under pressure
· Innovative leadership
· Situational leadership
· Flexible
· Strategic
· Visionary
· Entrepreneurial
· Charismatic

"Effective communication" could be another valuable qualification. Is your version best described by style or by area of expertise? Could you add any of the following characteristics to be more specific about your communication skills?

· Written and verbal
· Inspirational
· Precise, detailed
· Formal or informal
· Compassionate, analytical, strategic

Is another of your skills "positive human relations"? What does that mean for you? Try to describe your style and scope.

· Enthusiastic
· Sensitive
· For conflict management
· With diverse populations
· At all corporate levels

"Successful management" might be in relation to projects and programs. It might mean management of:

· Financial resources
· Human resources
· Processes
· Materials and inventories

So We Asked an Expert: Jodie Grubbs, Human Resources, Target Stores, says: "We look for analytical skills when hiring. We ask for specific examples and ask potential employees to explain their skills."

The Point: Analyze your skills as specifically as possible and show evidence of them in your achievements.

"Technical expertise," if that's one of your headlines, always needs to describe your special knowledge and to show your ongoing capacity for continued learning. What is the area of your expertise?

· Manufacturing processes
· Information systems
· Science, health, medical, other
· Languages
· Political, academic, corporate systems and protocols

Now you understand what we mean when we recommend that you create two to four headlines. They should grab attention and capture what you have to offer in just a few words.

3. Achievements: Examples of how your qualifications have resulted in past success

These will be brief, powerful stories showing evidence of the qualifications you've stated above. Each example will represent a problem or challenge you faced, the steps you took to meet it, and concrete results of your actions. Each of these stories should be an example of work—paid or unpaid—that you're proud of, the kind of work you would like to do in the future. Some achievements might be short-term; others may summarize a long-term endeavor. The choices must be yours, because only you can decide which stories most demonstrate the qualifications you want to offer.

Example 1: Achievements listed under "effective communications" could look like this if the writer is stressing both written and verbal skills at the same time:

> **Effective Communications:** *As volunteer publicist for a community health fair, I reviewed project files for past strategies, met with project leaders, and created a three-month plan. I solicited six volunteers, created a team, and delegated tasks. Tasks included strategy development, timeline management, brochure and poster production, and a media campaign. The project publicity resulted in highest-ever participation (10,000 attendees in two days). We created a permanent database of fifty volunteers for the future. Local news coverage included four print articles and three feature broadcasts on radio and television.*

Example 2: Another example to showcase communication skills while emphasizing analytical and strategic problem-solving might be:

> **Effective Communications:** *Increased employee complaints indicated the need to address and solve internal problems. I organized a lunchtime meeting and oversaw an issues-related brainstorming ses-*

sion. I directed others in helping identify three key issues related to work conditions. With management approval, short-term teams were formed to identify possible solutions. Team recommendations resulted in new employee policies to address and prevent future problems.

In both examples, we see a challenge, steps addressing that challenge, and concrete results. We have a statement of facts, short and straight to the point.

As you sort through and reflect on past achievements, pay particular attention to the patterns that arise. For example, you may find that you've been most successful at managing projects when the project was at least a year long. Or you might describe your "situational leadership" in relatively short-term projects, if those were your best achievements. The process of writing the Ah-ha résumé is not only for collecting and recording your best work but also for helping you understand the circumstances fostering your success.

4. Employment and Related Experience

This includes a list (present to past) of the settings in which your achievements have occurred. Where have you worked, when, and how? This section of the Ah-ha résumé will provide dates, jobs, and projects, along with titles or brief descriptions of roles you've held in each setting. (Don't assume that a prospective employer will be able to guess at the type of work you did just from the position title.) Paid and volunteer work can be interwoven, as long as each listing is an important part of your *achievement* history. If your summer job as a paper carrier in '78 isn't a big part of who you are now, leave it out. On the other hand, if the six-month temporary job you filled between career positions gave you the opportunity to develop your project management skills, by all means include it.

This section will most likely show, at a glance, that you've been active and employed and increasing your skills and abilities over many years. Younger people may want to include all past jobs, and the more experienced of you might leave off your earliest ones. Starting and ending dates should be indicated for jobs that lasted more than a year. If the years held multiple achievements in varied settings, however, you may list years and experiences in clusters. The focus, again, should be on your best achievements.

Example 1: Work and related experience for a midlife career person could create a richly condensed list.

- 1993–97: Heritage Family Insurance, Augusta, Georgia. Director of Sales and Marketing (1996–97), Account Manager (1994–96), Agent Coordinator (1993–94).
- 1994–95: Volunteer Coordinator, United Way of Augusta.
- 1990–97: Board of Directors, Georgia Risk Management Association.

Example 2: Work and related experience for an entry-level person could be listed in this manner:

- 1996–present: La Trip Travel Agency, Customer Service Representative, Champaign, Ill.
- 1995 semester: Study abroad program, Seville, Spain.
- 1994–96: Goofey's Pub, Seasonal Chef and Dining Room Host, Urbana, Ill.
- 1993–94: Caterer's assistant, Chez Moi, Decatur, Ill.

The idea is to show where you've worked and to suggest with a concise list that you've grown steadily in competence and levels of responsibility. So don't focus on the birth and death dates of the job as much as on the periods of achievement in your life and create a list that shows where you developed your skills.

5. Education and Training: Formal and professional education and training and other learning related to qualifications

This section will list in a fairly tight format your formal education and training as well as courses, conferences, or continuing education experiences that have added value to your qualifications. You may choose the order of listings, since older people might not emphasize a twenty-year-old degree, and younger graduates might choose to list recent degrees or certifications first. If you don't want to be specific about dates, you may omit them. But remember that in this era of life-long learning, year of graduation is not necessarily an indication of age.

Example 1: Somebody with recent formal credentials might list them as follows.

- B.A., Political Science, University of Wisconsin–Madison, 1989.
- Certificate, Kellogg Management Institute, Northwestern University, 1992.
- Continuing education courses in all aspects of marketing management, including surveys, promotions, direct mail, strategy development, 1990–96.
- Certification of completion, Community Leadership Seminar Series, Cambridge, Wis., 1996.

Example 2: Someone with less formal education could list:

- Proficiency in computer software programs, including Microsoft Word, Excel, Power Point, Access.
- Participation in training workshop in electronics (past five years), Leader Electronics, Laurel, Miss.
- Company mentoring program participant, Leader Electronics, Laurel, Miss. Selected as a mentor for 1997–98.

6. Projects, *Awards, Honors, and Other Experiences: Anything that highlights your qualifications and is not included in any other section*

What else is important to you? What else might interest an employer? Training for and completing a triathlon demonstrates strength, discipline, and endurance; these are valuable and marketable qualities. Listing your hobbies—golf, reading, hiking—does not generally tell anything new about your strengths, and it can make you sound amateurish. Note that we qualified that statement with "generally." If you're interested in management positions and you enjoy reading books on supervision, that's worth mentioning. If you like hiking so much that you've done the Appalachian Trail, that says something about you. The point: list the items that will help the reader see your strengths more clearly.

Examples:

· Completed annual Run Against Cancer marathon four consecutive years.
· Elected to Elks Executive Council, 1989–90.
· Appointed to Cleveland Economic Development Commission.
· Financed four-year undergraduate education while maintaining 3.5.
· Elected to Phi Beta Kappa, 1997.
· Captain, women's rugby team, Colby College, 1996.

These accomplishments, awards, and honors tell prospective employers something about you. They help complete the portrait.

▪ HOW THE AH-HA RÉSUMÉ WORKS ▪

Each section of your Ah-ha résumé will be a picture of you from a slightly different angle. Let's track the flow of information about you as it is presented in the Ah-ha résumé:

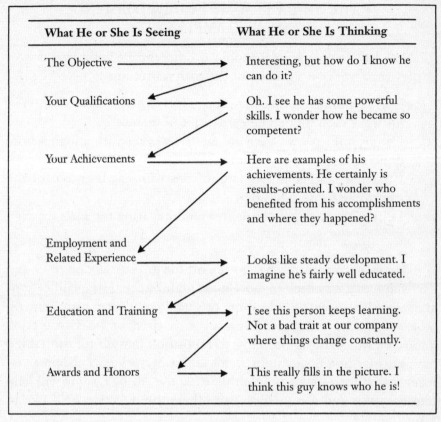

What He or She Is Seeing	What He or She Is Thinking
The Objective	Interesting, but how do I know he can do it?
Your Qualifications	Oh. I see he has some powerful skills. I wonder how he became so competent?
Your Achievements	Here are examples of his achievements. He certainly is results-oriented. I wonder who benefited from his accomplishments and where they happened?
Employment and Related Experience	Looks like steady development. I imagine he's fairly well educated.
Education and Training	I see this person keeps learning. Not a bad trait at our company where things change constantly.
Awards and Honors	This really fills in the picture. I think this guy knows who he is!

How an Ah-ha résumé stimulates a person to read it.

Perhaps the most important effect the Ah-ha résumé can have is to demonstrate

- Analytical skills—as you uncover the patterns of your accomplishments
- Organizational skills—as you create an orderly and readable document
- Communication skills—as you choose powerful, concise, and descriptive words to give specific insight
- Outcome focus—as you show that you are results-conscious and actually contribute to bottom-line success

▪ THE AH-HA RÉSUMÉ IN DEVELOPMENT: SOME EXAMPLES ▪

Now let's look at several people at different life and career stages as they each work on a section of their Ah-ha résumé.

- Darryl, a midlevel executive at age fifty, who lacks satisfaction in his work even though he earns a lot of money
- Danny, a thirty-two-year-old factory worker with a high school diploma and a lot of ambition
- Cristal, a mother in her late thirties who has been out of the workforce for several years
- Letitia, about to get her degree and preparing for a job search

Darryl, our executive, has gotten off the job satisfaction track and needs to find a way back to more meaningful work. His qualifications are: effective project leadership, profitable resource management, polished human relations. Because he is tired of his current job duties, he will write an objective to reposition himself for something new. He may find opportunity in his company, or he may begin a discreet search for a new job. In either case, the Ah-ha résumé will help him get clear and communicate to others the direction he'd like to take.

Darryl's objective will reflect this hope. He writes, "Seeking opportunity to lead new initiatives for profitable outcomes by collaborating with others." The objective is, for now, intentionally vague about the types of projects he would do. He isn't sure what's out there yet. But his objective clearly states his desire to lead, to do something new, and to work with others. And he is aiming for success, wherever it turns out to be.

Darryl knows that it's very important when creating an objective to match your desire with a positive result for others. It's never enough to indicate your wishes and desires without showing that you want to apply your talents for success of the organization or company. Darryl will go on to choose the best stories of his leadership, resource management, and human relations skills while demonstrating the times he started new projects and created a team approach.

Danny, our factory worker, never really thought of creating a résumé. He thought résumés were only for college graduates or the folks upstairs in the executive suite. So Danny needs to work to identify his qualifications for the first time. On the job for the past ten years, he's been given increased responsibility, moving up from line work to supervision. He's gained technical skills in running machinery and in improving manufacturing processes. He'd really like to be considered for management of a department and would need to be selected for his company's management training program to move upward toward his goal.

Meanwhile, outside of work Danny's been active in organizing an athletic program for young girls in the community. The father of an eight-year-old daughter, Danny has worked to bring other interested parents together, gone to the city recreation department for funding, and organized the first under-ten girls' softball league. He even helped out when a flyer had to be written and sent to a large number of parents. So, while Danny's work experience has given him several strong qualifications—technical expertise, supervisory skills, systems improvement—he can now add project management to his list and include it as a résumé qualification.

When he writes out his achievement to display this strength, he will succinctly describe what he did and the results:

> *I led in the creation of a first-ever citywide girls-under-ten soft-ball league. I organized parents in a series of meetings to establish interest and commitment. We met with recreational planning committee members to create a budget and proposal, which was then funded. I helped write and distribute flyers with team member applications. We formed teams, created a season schedule, and recruited parent-coaches.*
>
> *Results: sixty third- and fourth-grade girls competed in twenty-nine games over ten weeks. The city has extended funding for next year.*

When Danny completes his Ah-ha résumé, it will demonstrate that he is worthy of the special training that will put him on the management track at work.

Cristal, a former nurse, is ready to reenter the workforce after several years of being home with her children. The Ah-ha résumé will be very useful to her because she dreads the thought of going back to conventional nursing after the years of flexibility she has enjoyed. As Cristal looks back over the time she's shared with her children and experienced in the community, she discovers that her qualifications have actually broadened. Volunteer projects have polished her communication skills. She still has great interest in health-related issues, but she wants to combine her background in nursing with her growing communication skills. Her objective might read, "Seeking opportunity to combine technical health care background in a community education setting using presentation skills to reach targeted populations effectively."

Cristal's qualifications will spotlight her health care experience and communication skills equally. She will give examples of achievements from work settings and projects over the past several years in her role as a community volunteer. Her section on Work and Related Experience will include those projects as if they had been paid employment. For example:

- 1996–98: Program chair for Shaker Heights Middle School annual fund-raiser.
- 1995–97: Parent volunteer for annual Healthy Teen Week.

Letitia has no idea what she wants to be. She'll soon have a degree in psychology and knows only that she wants to get a job where she can continue to learn about organizations and how they develop. She is also interested in social causes and people who work to help others. Her jobs have been conventional for her age: retail, office work, a few campus jobs with special events. She spent one semester as an intern in a family services agency. As she looks back, she's most proud of a mentoring program she helped establish in her dorm to help "at risk" high school girls.

Letitia's objective will say, "Seeking opportunity to combine strong learning goals and psychology background in a human services setting in need of vital, committed professional." Pretty lyrical, but Letitia wants to offer her energy enthusiastically and indicate clearly that she's still learning but ready to work.

Letitia will be able to list several items under Special Achievements and Awards. She has been a campus leader, has volunteered enough hours to win a citation, and holds office in her dorm council. These are special notations that show who she is and help the reader of her résumé fill in the picture of an active new graduate who seeks to continue learning.

The next chapters will focus on the incremental development of various strategies for exploring your goals and new directions. The more you add to and improve your Ah-ha résumé, the richer it will become as a multiuse resource. In addition to depending on it as you prepare for interviews and then as a point of reference during interviews, the most important function of the Ah-ha résumé will be the thinking and writing you do to create it. Your goals, your headlines, your stories with their results, the tight lists of jobs, education, and achievements—all will combine to paint a self-portrait of surprising value.

ACTION STEPS FOR BUILDING YOUR AH-HA RÉSUMÉ

1. Draw a LifeCircle and make certain you have fully explored each quadrant of your life for your best achievements. Assemble your notes from previous chapters for easy access. Your Ah-ha résumé will be the source of the strategies you use to move forward.

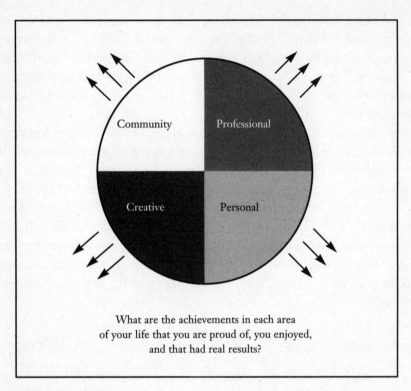

LifeCircle: Achievements.

2. Begin a draft of your Ah-ha résumé. Plan on spending several sessions and plenty of paper or computer time to complete all the steps. Use the following format for general direction, but don't limit the length during the development of each section.

Figure 6–6.   Ah-ha Résumé Form

Name
Address
Phone

Objective:

Qualifications:
•

•

•

Achievements:
•

•

•

•

Employment and Related Experience:

Education and Training:

Awards and Honors:
•

•

•

•

seven

What's What Networking

Anthony, a friend of ours in Washington, D.C., was interested in the possibility of starting his own consulting practice. To explore the idea, he asked three friends for suggestions of people he could talk to. Each person he asked gave him three or four names. He contacted ten of the people recommended and scheduled a meeting with each one. At every meeting he gained additional contacts. By the end of the second week of "networking," Anthony phoned to say he had met with forty-three people. What should he do now? We told him to take a cold shower and wear a sign that said, "Stop me before I network again!"

▪ THE OLD NETWORKING: WHO'S WHO ▪

Networking, a buzzword for the past decade or so, can provide a rich structure for finding information, insight, and opportunity—or it can become a sticky web with random strands stretched in too many directions. There was a time (the year "network" became a verb) when ambitious and energetic people raced from work to church, to community events, to art openings, to cocktail parties, scattering business cards all along the way. And we collected as many as we distributed. Back then we pumped hands, smiled brightly, promised to get in touch, and tried to be sincere—when we could remember whom we saw and where we were—as if we were politicians the week before an election.

What was our goal? What had we expected? To make good contacts? Once in a while it happened, but the odds were only slightly better than winning at casino bingo. (Mostly you lose, sometimes you get a turkey, and every so often you sit next to someone who wins big. But they almost never help you fill your bingo card.) Perhaps we thought we'd be "discovered" at the events we networked. But who was out there to discover us? And what did we really want from them?

Eventually, many of us were able to insulate our houses with the cards we collected. We couldn't remember most of the people we'd met, so the least we could do was make sure they had positive environmental impact.

That was the essence of the old networking, the "who's who" approach to making connections. Fortunately, there's something better now.

▪ A NEW APPROACH—WHAT'S WHAT NETWORKING ▪

"What's what" networking offers a perspective for connecting with people in a meaningful context. It's not frenzied; it's careful. In this chapter you'll focus on understanding the scope of opportunities (knowledge, advice, advocacy, important connections) that can be found in using or building a network. You'll look at approaches you can use to broaden your network, based not on whom you know but on what information you need and what you want to offer to others. You'll consider opportunities to become a genuine resource and demonstrate your value in real and memorable ways. If the "who's who" networking of the past was built on sheer activity, the "what's what" networking is appropriate for our busy lives today because it's built on strategy.

Dictionary definitions of "strategy" refer to military advantage achieved cleverly, cunningly. Some people might consider a "cunning" career strategy an advantage. The career advice we *don't* recommend is the kind that offers general strategies for a military-like career advantage with no regard for the individual who must carry out and live with the results of the conquest. (What if you win the Falklands?

Do you really have time on your Lifeline to deal with managing a bunch of islands and flocks of sheep?)

Finding a "killer career advantage" isn't the same as finding "the best work of your life." For our purposes, we'll rely on Webster's secondary definition of strategy as "that which is of great, vital importance within an integrated whole." Strategy, in this sense, *takes into account the important parts of your life to create a career advantage*. The continual process of gaining *clarity* emphasizes knowing who you are from a number of perspectives and identifying what you need at each stage of your life. Building a *strategy* means communicating your strengths (as they become clear to you) to those who want or need the best work you can do.

What you'll need for building your strategy will be a strong and effective résumé and the ability to understand, identify, and initiate opportunity for your life and work. If you leave out parts of the whole, there will be no integration between who you are, what you want, and what you get. A successfully integrated strategy will become a meaningful plan to drive your actions. *Actions* will provide a menu of resources for moving your strategy forward.

▪ A LOOK AT STRATEGIC THINKING IN GENERAL ▪

Let's stay focused on strategy for a while. The philosophy of this book and of our work with individuals is based on a strategic, whole-person approach. We try to get people, including you, in the habit of asking questions such as "Why *am I* doing this? How *can I* do it better? What do *I really want*?"

Why do we ask these questions? They help people focus on taking control and staying honest with themselves about the decisions they make. In contrast, a nonstrategic approach to career issues would pay too much attention to questions such as "What am I *supposed* to do? How do *others want me* to behave? What *should* I be doing?" This kind of thinking might force you to offer only the part of yourself you think fits the view of others. With an integrated strategy, you can actually offer much more. And you're more likely to get what meets your needs. That's the point of all this.

Strategy: Some Examples

In the course of a recent day we received calls from five clients. Each one had a different career-related concern and wanted some advice. Here's what happened:

Winnie was ambivalent about a job opportunity at a health care center. Her résumé, a traditional listing of previous positions, wasn't bad. But her understanding of the importance of her achievements was missing. Our "strategic" advice for her was to create an analytical, skill-based résumé for greater self-understanding. She did this, then called to say she had a "breakthrough" experience and realized that the advantages she could offer might set her apart from other applicants. She became more interested in the job when she realized how her qualifications could make it an interesting opportunity.

Adrian, a talented restaurateur, called to say he'd been fired from his new position as a chef after only two weeks. A nonstrategic approach in his situation would have been simply to hammer at the marketplace aggressively for another job. Our strategic advice, however, was to encourage him to take another look at his personal history, which was marked by lifelong creative achievements, and to review his work history for patterns that represented his best skills, work preferences, and strengths.

For most of his career Adrian had owned a restaurant. It became apparent to him that adapting to the culture of other owners was a new challenge, one he had not met successfully in his most recent job. Why not seek out opportunities that would take advantage of his creative genius in a setting that could tolerate his independent nature? He spoke with several headhunters in New York who specialize in staffing expensive restaurants. Once Adrian could articulate his strengths and preferences, they began uncovering opportunities well within the salary range for someone with his level of expertise. Two of them identified professional settings they believed would welcome his independence and would thrive as a result. He was able to turn a perceived weakness—his inability to subordinate himself—into a strategic advantage by honoring his personality and his work history.

Connie called to discuss opportunities for reentry into a professional marketing career. She admitted she was really hoping we could provide "placement" or significant contacts. As we became acquainted on the phone, we learned that she had just gone through a long period of caregiving for her mother, who had recently passed away. Connie was still finishing up some family-related details but felt it was time to reenter the workforce. She talked at length about all she'd learned from managing her mother's care. She wished others could understand the natural process of an elderly person dying, as she had, and come to see the experience of caregiving in a positive light. She had taken a leave from her career and realized that she was very fulfilled by the job of managing her mother's last years. We encouraged Connie to create new visions for work based on her recent life stage experiences. By applying her marketing skills in a health care or social service setting, she might be able to leverage newly acquired insights into a job serving families in need of resources to deal with the complexities and rewards of caregiving.

Michelle, a young client just out of graduate school, called to say she was having a crisis of confidence in San Francisco. After five weeks she still hadn't found a job related to public policy, her specialty. Because financial status and risk tolerance are highly individual matters, we talked about her resources and her frame of mind. She needed income fast but was willing to take a "temp" job to support her continuing career search, and she was moderately comfortable with the risk involved in "keeping the faith." We presented the LifeCircle to Michelle as a means to explore sources of opportunity. It occurred to her that her membership in her undergrad alumni association gave her access to a national alumnae network. The San Francisco branch was about to hold a mentoring evening. She had just enough time to request a directory of alumnae in the area so she could quickly identify which ones to approach for future informational interviews. Suddenly, the world started looking brighter in the City by the Bay. Michelle continued to develop a personal networking strategy rather than sidetrack her goals and lose the career vision she'd begun forming in graduate school.

Lisa was excited when she called. The art school in Seattle had just announced an opening in an administrative area of interest to her. The job description was posted, and she wanted to apply. But there was a problem. She had just begun taking courses in graphic design, and if she were chosen for the job, she'd have to give them up. As Lisa described the job tasks, it became apparent that she would be involved with the graphic arts in a variety of ways in the new position. Could she set some learning goals while taking on a new job? Would the school allow (perhaps support) her continuing interest in this related area? Might her interest in graphics even be perceived as an advantage to those who would interview her? She decided to create a strategy that would incorporate her interest with her learning goals in her application for the job.

Each of these clients created a "next step" in his or her career development by identifying and using a personal perspective for strategic change, rather than moving forward without a plan. It is critical to rethink and reintegrate information continuously in order to take advantage of opportunity or lessons learned through disappointments (getting demoted or fired, not earning a promotion) as you move toward your best work. It's important to understand that we can seek opportunity to refine our plans, our work, our next visions.

We don't have to become a round peg just because the holes are round. The strategy is simple. Bring yourself and your priorities along as your career moves forward. Change the shape of the space in which you will fit by making it bigger.

▪ WHAT'S WHAT NETWORKING: STRATEGY IN ACTION ▪

Knowing what's what about the information you need is the only way to take advantage of strategic networking. After Anthony cooled down from his networking frenzy, we advised him to retrace his steps and spend time recapturing the "what's what"—information he'd gained—from the who's who of Washington consultants. His well-meaning friends had put him in touch with a number of knowledgeable people. He'd probably even gained valuable information but lost track of it. He certainly had plenty of referrals for the future. It was time to see if he could assemble a strategy, at least in a backward fashion. What had he gained in forty-three meetings, and how did it fit with what he needed and what he still needs to know?

We advised him to begin by temporarily forgetting that he had met with anyone. His first task was to devise a career strategy based on what information he needed. We told him then to recall each interview and fill in the blanks to recapture his valuable but unfocused experience.

Anthony decided there are several goals you can have in seeking to meet with someone who knows what's what.

1. Immediate response and feedback about how you present yourself
2. Specific advice about a chosen subject in his or her area of expertise
3. Advice about how you should proceed in your exploration
4. Stories about his or her career path and professional decision-making
5. Observations of his or her professional persona, work style, and values
6. Information about professional opportunity pertinent to you
7. Names of additional people who know what's what in relation to your next area of exploration

In approaching his interviews strategically, Anthony realized several things. The first was that he had wasted a good deal of time asking the same questions and getting similar answers. The next realization was truly a rude awakening. Anthony had underutilized several opportunities by meeting too soon with people who might have been better resources later as his career search became more refined. For example, he'd met with an exciting young man who does most of his work in eastern Europe in social policy development. Anthony remembered, with considerable discomfort, that he'd asked the man mostly about where he'd gone to school and how he'd begun his practice. In retrospect, Anthony could have learned a great deal from the man about the international market for someone with his skills.

Sometimes, as we search for new career information or directions, we are given the name of someone with unusual expertise, such as the eastern Europe–based consultant. A rule to remember in networking is that we rarely get a chance for a second interview. The busiest people are frequently willing to set aside fifteen or twenty minutes to see someone referred by an associate. But if you try to see them again, they may feel that you've taken advantage of the contact. A second approach implies a relationship, obligations. You'll be unlikely to get a second chance. (There will be more information on protocols in the next chapter.)

As Anthony reviewed his meeting notes, he realized that he had acquired information about starting a business, advice about business decisions in the consulting field, marketing insights, even some direct money talk about potential earnings. All good information.

But he had failed to get any strategic advice, because he hadn't created a strategy. He had formed a few assumptions based on his observations about the pace of consulting, the nature of the work, and the environment in which it happens. He wished desperately that he could go back and listen and observe with more focused attention.

He made up his mind to create a genuine strategy for further exploration and to use the newest referrals wisely. He realized now that he needs to seek vital information that will be "a part of the whole" picture he is trying to paint for possible opportunities.

We sometimes refer to the situation in which Anthony got caught up as "flat-circle networking." Standing in one place, he spun around in a large circle, collecting information that became layered over other information until he couldn't remember where he started or what the layers radiating around him meant.

Imagine, instead, creating a spiral of information in which you begin to move carefully and thoroughly around, while at the same time advancing upward by building information as you go. You are still at the center, but you're able to filter and refine the information to get what you need. Each turn of your spiral brings you to a better view of "what's what."

A good place to begin developing your strategy is to look at your Me/Now position in combination with your Ah-ha résumé and ask yourself:

· What are my strongest qualifications—the strengths I bring to my best work?
· What are my parameters, my goals for my next career phase? (You may not know exactly what you want to do, but you should be clear about what you do best.)

· What are my preferences for how I'd like to work in the future? (You've spent time analyzing both your past successes and your future needs, so you should be able to at least imagine some directions to explore.)
· What companies or organizations seem worth exploring? What professions or industries would provide a match for my skills? (These are questions you will be able to refine through networking and through independent research, but it will help if you start with a few ideas of your own.)

When you've had a chance to look at the whole picture of who you are and what you already know about yourself, what you don't know will be more obvious. As you read the last section of this book, you'll find that there is an abundance of information you can acquire independently. There are other pieces of the whole picture you can only get through strategic networking: feedback about your strengths, ideas about how they might be used in the workplace, and specific information about a particular person's career. Seek personal advice, dig for career-related stories, develop perceptions through observation, acquire knowledge about opportunities, and ask for the names of people to speak with in the future. Seek, dig for, develop, acquire, ask for—all active verbs. We direct the networking interview because we are directing our career.

So We Asked an Expert. Pam Wegner, Vice President, Information Technology and Administration, Wisconsin Power and Light, says: "When I meet someone who would be an excellent resource for the company but there is no official position open, I may bring him or her in to talk to a group of people and try to develop some kind of entree for them in the organization to see if something can develop."

The Point: If managers believe a person can add value to the organization, they will work hard to find a job for this individual.

▪ IDENTIFY YOUR NETWORK ▪

Not everyone has the contacts Anthony did. His friends were connected to people "in the know" who eagerly provided him with the names of other informed professionals. But what if you don't know where to begin, much less how to manage a full calendar of interviews?

Start with your LifeCircle. Use the LifeCircle to begin to identify people who might be able to help you gather the information you need to develop your career opportunities. Remember: it's not *who you know* that's important, it's *what they know.*

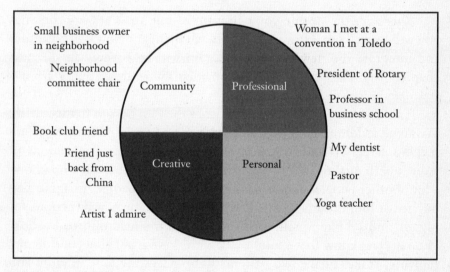

LifeCircle: People who know "what's what."

Professional	Those in your work setting or related industries who understand what's going on, who are aware of industry challenges, trends, and influences that will shape future opportunities. Find the decision-makers, resource-getters, and those who have positive influence with others.
Community	People who are committed to issues, leaders in problem-solving, who demonstrate vision, opportunity, compassion, discipline. Find people who can help you learn more about issues important to you, local or global.

Personal	Think about the people who seem to know what you need to know next, those who are accomplished and effective in living their lives. Find people who are not like you, who can teach you directly or subtly about different ways to grow.
Creative	Seek out the visionaries here, too—those whose music or art can inspire, those with whom you'd want to share a desert island. Find the ones who can make you laugh or cry or lose all track of time. Find a poet, a rock star, a minister, a Buddhist priest, a gardener, a comedian, an elder.

These are the people you will want to talk to. They are the ones you will learn from. How you'll approach them and how you'll capture and integrate the new insights you gain will be covered in the next chapter. Right now, the focus is on identifying opportunity from a strategic perspective.

If all else fails, choose your dentist as the first person to meet with. We aren't kidding. As soon as you can explain comfortably that you are seeking career-related direction about new or better applications of your superb qualifications, you can begin with one person who knows a lot of other people. Dentists know hundreds of people. Imagine asking her or him this question: "I'm thinking of some new directions for myself, and I'd like to talk with someone in the field of broadcasting. Who do you know that I might talk with?" Now imagine your dentist replying, "Gee. I have two patients in broadcasting, one in radio and one in TV. I'd be happy to connect you."

See? It's not hard to begin, even if you have to start with your dentist, your hairdresser, or your clergy person.

Create or Join a Network

Consider existing opportunities to join ready-made networks that you can find in professional organizations, church committees, neighborhood associations, political campaigns, fund-raising groups, book discussion clubs, and so on. If you're interested in getting to know people with specific professional qualifications, aim for a group of your peers. If you're interested in exploring new markets for your work, think of professions that could use the kinds of skills you have to offer.

You should choose networks strategically. For example, if you're a professional marketer, marketing association members will provide industry insights but will very likely have the same challenges you do. On the other hand, by joining a broader-based business organization, you'll learn more about future "customers." Choose your networks according to your strategy. Understand what you want to learn, and the appropriate network will become apparent.

Some of our best strategic networking has come from networks that we've created. A group of neighbors meets monthly to discuss the pleasures and pitfalls of working out of a home-based office. There are two computer wizards, one graphic designer, one noted children's author, a columnist, a poet, and an academic specializing in Spanish literary erotica. As we've developed our career management business, we've gained critical feedback and advice from members of this group.

Early in our business development, we realized that two other women we knew were developing high-level business ventures, each completely different from our own. We formed a small network we named The Associates. We christened our group with just a bit of humor (as in "My associates insist that I raise my rates this year"). We meet for dinner bimonthly and discuss business progress, triumphs, and travails. We talk over proposals, planning, and contract negotiations, and we exchange advice about upcoming career decisions. We've developed a great affection for our small network, and we've set some serious professional standards from our discussions.

We each have different areas of expertise, and the people we know through our business specialties are quite diverse. We're able to offer contacts and referrals to one another without reservation. While this is not informational networking in the sense of Anthony's experience, it is strategic in nature and is a network of our own invention. The Associates have added professional quality to our lives and a sense of balance through warm, business-related friendships.

Contribute to a Network and It Will Become Your Own

As you develop opportunities for short-term networking, consider the ways in which you could become involved on a longer-term basis with networks by engaging in shared activities. Again, your LifeCircle can be your guide. Recall the achievements you've added up in each area of your life and assess possible new involvements. Remember to keep your "best work" in mind. Look at each quadrant of the circle and use your imagination.

1. **Professional.** How can I cross over into another work project or department to increase my involvement and apply my strengths in a new way? What conference could I attend to meet people I've never met before? What class could I take to learn a skill that would strengthen my qualifications?
2. **Personal.** What if I started a new fitness regimen at the Y? I could meet new people and get into better shape. Maybe I could help organize the annual charity run, too. I'm going to take the class on literacy instruction at the high school. Then I'll be able to offer help in a new way to others. We should join a cooking class or gourmet club. Our relationship could use the attention and we haven't met new friends in years.
3. **Community.** I'd like to help with the neighborhood long-range planning committee; I know just what I could offer. I wonder if there's a way to reach out to the family that had that terrible fire and lost everything. I think I'll talk to the pastor this week and try to get something started. I'd really like to be considered for appointment to one of the mayor's committees. I'll call city hall tomorrow and try to find out how to get into their resource pool.
4. **Creative.** Everybody golfs. I think I'll join a tai chi class. I'm giving myself until June 14 to finish that article I started; I'll have it in the mail on the twentieth. I'm going to ask two or three of my friends to look it over and give me their reactions before I send it off.

We've been astonished to learn during the past year of the secret "creative" lives of two professional women in our neighborhood. One,

So We Asked an Expert. Linda Bohman, Human Resources Director, Virchow Krause and Co., states: "You can develop a meaningful professional network by getting involved with professional associations and civic groups outside of work. Stay in touch with your classmates. Go to association meetings and get involved in leadership roles. Stay in touch with people who leave the organization, and stay in touch if you leave."

The Point: Think broadly about your networks. Stay proactive, connected, and dynamic.

a psychotherapist, revealed during a potluck dinner with neighbors that she is an award-winning Latin dancer who performs and competes nationally. Another, a local gallery owner, has just returned from scaling Mount Kilimanjaro and has been quietly leading women's adventure trips for years.

Most of these examples are not direct career moves. But they are career-building activities. If you start a new activity that involves or improves your best skills and strengths in a new network, you will gain:

· Access to new people
· New confidence
· New enthusiasm
· New ideas
· Possible new directions to explore

These are the building blocks for a healthy continuing career plan. As you find new directions and new networks, you will be strategically supporting your habit of Clarity, Strategy, and Action.

▪ CONTINUING EVOLUTION OF YOUR AH-HA RÉSUMÉ ▪

So how is your Ah-ha résumé evolving? Where are you in your journey of self-discovery and career progress?

Objective. Still general at this point.

Qualifications. You may be refining them as you think of new ways to apply your skills.

Achievements. Continue selecting the most powerful ones from past experience. Begin to identify strategically those you would like to feature for specific new opportunities. Keep nonwork achievements prominent in networking conversations, to present a full picture of yourself and to remain open for feedback and new direction.

Work and Related Experience. Tighten the format of your list. Get feedback on your mix of professional and nonprofessional experiences.

Education and Training. Continue to review your work and related history for all structured learning. Begin to imagine how you would like to continue your lifelong learning.

Special Achievements and Awards. Consider adding an achievement by contributing your skills in a new setting while developing a new network.

ACTION STEPS FOR BUILDING YOUR WHAT'S WHAT NETWORK

1. Continue developing your résumé according to the suggestions above.
2. Think back through the various kinds of contacts you've made in the past year with people whom you could describe as knowing "what's what." Did you learn anything from them that has influenced your career strategy? Could you? Are they people you could approach in the future?
3. Using your LifeCircle as a focal point, note the names of everyone you can think of for each quadrant who might be someone "in the know." Begin to make a list of these people and make preliminary notes about what you think you could learn from them in relation to your career.
4. Make sure you understand what "strategy" means to you before moving on to the next chapter. The upcoming protocols and suggestions for mapping and tracking opportunity will be useful only if you know how to apply what you learn.

eight

Mapping and Tracking Opportunity

▪ GIVING PEOPLE A CHANCE TO HELP ME ▪

Why would anyone want to help me? Because people like helping other people. There's no question about it. We all have times in our lives when we are able to be of genuine service to another at a critical moment. We offer just the right advice, make a perfect suggestion, or listen with concerned attention. When we do this, we feel good about ourselves; we feel resourceful and strong. And we feel invested in a positive outcome for the person we are helping. We want to know how they are getting along, what decisions they've made, and whether or not we were a genuine influence on their progress. We have a sense of advocacy for the person who asks for *and* uses our help.

A powerful approach for building advocacy, gaining knowledge, and expanding a network of additional contacts is the informational/referral interview. If you're curious about a new direction but you haven't focused on anything specific, meet with people who can provide referrals to help you find those "in the know." When you've focused on an area that interests you, move into interviews with people who can give you more information about work or job opportunities.

Whether your purpose for an interview is to seek referrals, information, or both, one of the most valuable resources we can have in professional and career-related situations is the goodwill of those who know things we need to learn or who are in a position to advise us concerning our best interests.

It is necessary not only to understand who these people might be but to know how to approach them respectfully and with a sense of purpose. Allowing, even inviting, another to help you implies that you will take responsibility for identifying your specific need for their help. You must understand your situation and know why a particular individual is the right person to approach. Your strategic perspective is based on clarity about your life and work, and clarity about what you have to know next in order to progress up the networking spiral.

▪ TAKING CONTROL ▪

The thrust of our book so far has been to encourage you to get and maintain control over your career. Self-direction is the only way to find and engage in the best work of your life. We've counseled ambitious, creative people who have become so autonomous that they refuse to seek advice or even hear the shouts of those who want to help them. The philosophy of managing your career does not preclude asking for help from others and using what they're able to offer.

The help you seek and the ways in which you use it need to be of your design. The point is to be self-motivated, to develop a personal vision for your career and life, then to add to it by recognizing the special people all around you who can help you enrich your future.

Supplicants and Applicants

Do you remember a time when you sat face-to-face in a professional setting and felt like a supplicant? Do you remember a time when you felt you were, in a sense, begging for an opportunity? It might have been at a job interview, during a performance review, or at a time when you were trying to present a new idea and needed the support of the person before you. Uncomfortable, wasn't it?

Now, think about a time when you were in a somewhat better position, still seeking something, but as an applicant. Maybe you were applying for a position, an opportunity, and you just waited, hoping to qualify, to be chosen. Stressful, wasn't it? Maybe you felt like one of the actors auditioning for *A Chorus Line* who had just danced and sung your heart out, then stood there sweating and squinting into a dark auditorium, hoping there was somebody out there, hoping you would get the part.

Director of Your Career

We strongly encourage you, now and forever, to give up the roles of both supplicant and applicant. A solid alternative can be found in taking on the perspective of *director* of your career. If you present yourself as one who is directing your life and work, you will always be in a position of both giving and getting information in order to maintain clarity in your decisions.

Instead of begging (supplicating), you will present what you have to offer, described in a clear, truthful, and persuasive manner. You'll describe your value and encourage a response that dignifies your request.

Instead of waiting to be chosen (as an applicant), you will showcase your best performances in exact relation to the role requirements. If you're smart, you'll have questions for the "casting agents" because, in a sense, you are also auditioning them, and you must find agreement to go into production.

As you become the director of your life and career, you will establish an appropriate level of authority over your life. As long as you maintain this sense of authority, you're more likely to find what you need and to feel better about the search process. If you lose this sense of authority, you'll slip back into subordinate positions that undermine the very strengths you are trying to present.

All this will take some thinking and reframing on your part. Practice getting into character by revisiting your Lifeline, your Ah-ha résumé, and your LifeCircle to authenticate, again and again, all that you are, all that you've done, and all that you have to offer.

Once you've coached yourself successfully into a balanced, self-directing frame of mind, then you can identify what you don't yet know and will need to learn from others. Imagine (and truly visualize) reaching out to others from a center of your authority but with equal respect for theirs. Now you're getting ready to meet those who know "what's what."

▪ INFORMATIONAL/REFERRAL INTERVIEWS: REASONS ▪

Many people seem to resist doing informational/referral interviews. Why do we strongly recommend them? Because they work. From this sort of interview you can gain greater clarity about your qualifications and possible career directions. You can also get some suggestions about whom you should contact next for further direction. And you can start a relationship that can be valuable in many ways. A great example of what an informational/referral interview can do came to us from a university administrator.

I met an outstanding student in an interview several years ago. Renata, a business major, was very ambitious and was looking for any opportunity for volunteer projects. I liked her immediately and wanted to help. She assisted me with a few small tasks over the next semester. By the following fall, I couldn't resist hiring her as an intern. She was not only a help but an added resource. She was calm in the midst of hectic activity. The more she did, the better I liked her. I kept increasing her responsibilities until she was in charge of a major project. She was to conduct research, write, and develop print materials on her own. We kept a running dialogue about the project, her work style, and her developing vision for an after-college career.

My desire to help Renata grew, and I engaged in greater advocacy. In time, I made sure she accompanied me on a trip east to meet with a financial company doing business with us. This company eventually hired her, based on my enthusiastic recommendation, which was inspired by her talent and proven competence.

I still get wonderful reports from her about her job, and she still thanks me every time I get together with her current manager. I also get some good-humored kidding about how self-directed Renata is, how she has requested and received increasing responsibility. She continues to be very much in charge of her career strategy. She earned my advocacy from the beginning and has kept it, and I continue to take pride in her success.

Ꭶ Ꭶ Ꭶ

How many success stories like this are out there? Who knows? But they don't just happen. You've got to have a strategy, to know what you want and what you need, then find people who can help and build relationships with them.

▪ INFORMATIONAL/REFERRAL INTERVIEWS: GAINING OR LOSING ADVOCACY ▪

The phone just rang. The caller was a woman from Chicago who wondered if we would have time to see her tomorrow. We don't. We're quite busy, but we are generally happy to arrange a brief meeting with anyone who gives us enough lead time. Unfortunately, this was not the case here.

Another caller, earlier this morning, began by requesting a brief response to an idea she had. One of us gladly spent ten minutes on the phone with her strategizing for an upcoming presentation she is planning.

Our response to such requests depends on our availability but also on a caller's ability to focus on his or her need in a way we can relate to. We wanted to help both callers, but the first person made it impossible by not giving us advance notice, while the second made it easy by offering us a chance to be helpful in a quick, time-limited way. We can never resist that kind of opportunity. Like anyone else, we like to provide assistance to others.

Unfortunately, not always being able to help is a condition of modern life, particularly for people who know "what's what." There are times when others want their help or advice, and they can't give it because they're just unavailable—too busy, too fragmented, or too consumed by priorities. But sometimes—and this is most frustrating—they would like to be of assistance but the person seems to make it difficult, impossible, or too unpleasant to earn and keep their advocacy. Consider the following example.

A busy corporate executive described the many types of requests he gets from people seeking informational interviews. He always tries to say yes, not only because he finds such interactions stimulating but because he feels a commitment to helping people.

He has some definite preferences, however, in the ways he likes to be approached. He prefers to get a brief note in advance from people wanting to schedule interviews, particularly if they have specific questions for him or certain issues they hope to explore. This gives him a chance to think about their interests and to guess at the amount of time the interview will take. He is generally able to meet with someone for only ten or fifteen minutes, and he likes to use the time well, in a focused manner. He also prefers it when the person follows up the note with a call to schedule a meeting. It's most helpful if the individual specifies in the note when he or she will call, so he can alert his secretary in advance and ask her to schedule an appointment when the call comes. These are the right things to do, the things that make it easy and enjoyable for this executive to help.

What almost never works, however, is when someone just drops in hoping he'll be available for a few minutes. Even when he is, he admits he harbors an underlying sense of irritation over the lack of advance planning and the implication that his time isn't valuable. Anyone perceived as inconsiderate is less likely to benefit fully from this contact. Being unprofessional is not a good beginning for gaining his advocacy or ongoing interest.

Another example to make this point: A professor relates that she frequently meets with students to help them with career strategies. A particular frustration for her, though, is the absence of an agenda. There is nothing more discouraging than scheduling a meeting with a student who then just sits there and doesn't take control of the situation. She's actually had a student say, "You start"—as if the professor had been doing nothing but thinking about this student's career since he made the appointment, as if the professor were responsible for this student's career. Of course, she could unload a ton of good, general information on anyone, but she doesn't want to spend her time or theirs in such an unfocused manner.

On the other hand, she really responds well when a student begins by saying something like "I have three questions and would love any additional perspectives you could give me, particularly if you think I'm overlooking questions I should be asking." This kind of an approach is the perfect balance of self-direction and openness that makes for a great meeting.

Both the executive and the professor find it offensive if people who approach them have only general questions, the kind that could and should be researched through information sources other than personal interview time. The very best questions are the ones individuals have thought about in advance and that relate specifically to the experience or expertise of the person being interviewed. Both of these professionals truly enjoy hearing people talk about their strengths and skills. It allows them the opportunity to give specific feedback and advice.

These two examples should give you some ideas about how to approach people for informational/referral interviews. The main points to remember here:

· Show consideration for the other person.
· Convey a sense of purpose when asking to schedule a meeting.
· Be prepared: find out everything you can from other sources, then be ready with questions.
· Direct the meeting to meet your needs and to make it easier for the other person to engage in advocacy.

If you approach informational/referral interviews with the right strategy and the right protocol, you're more likely to get what you need—information and referrals, as well as an advocate.

▪ INFORMATIONAL/REFERRAL INTERVIEWS: PROTOCOL ▪

In these stories about interviews we can find useful guidelines about what to do and what not to do. Much of it may seem to be common sense, but our experience as career consultants has shown us that common sense may not be that common after all, particularly in unfamiliar situations. Here's a good protocol to follow in setting up and conducting such interviews:

· Approach people courteously to request a meeting.
· Be prompt for appointments.
· Identify and state the reasons why you believe their perspective is unique and valuable for you.
· Prepare for your interview: find out whatever you can from other sources, so you're more knowledgeable.

· Create an agenda with a few key questions.
· Be open to additional ideas and information.
· Listen carefully.
· Ask questions if you don't understand or if you want to know more.
· Take notes.
· Be able to describe succinctly your key qualifications and any appropriate achievements. (Notice the adverb and adjectives here: *succinctly, key, appropriate.*)

As your focus sharpens, ask who else he or she would suggest that you contact. Then do the following.

· Ask for permission to use his or her name as a referral.
· Reflect back on the key points you've gained during the interview.
· Promise to keep the person you've met with informed as your career planning develops.
· Write a thank-you note immediately and be specific about the benefits you gained from your time together. Again, state why you found his or her perspective unique and valuable.

And although we'd like to think that the following guideline doesn't need to be stated:

· Dress appropriately for the situation, most often business attire and good shoes. Always be well groomed. If you visit an environment where suits aren't necessary, still pay attention to your clothes and appearance. How you present yourself makes a difference in how people perceive you. Never apologize for a casual or sloppy appearance. Never have a reason to do so. We've emphasized throughout this book that you've got to be yourself, but here we're reminding you to show proper consideration for the people with whom you meet.

▪ INFORMATIONAL/REFERRAL INTERVIEWS: RESULTS ▪

Much of the above discussion has been about what we should do to create successful opportunities. The focus has necessarily been on the people we want to meet and learn from. Step back to your Lifeline for a moment. Stand firmly on the Me/Now spot. How has an informational or referral interview changed your position?

If you've been thinking strategically, the information you've gained should help fill in a few unknowns. You've learned about the career path of another person, his or her choice of industry, and specific insights provoked by your questions. You might have been privy to certain hopes and dreams he or she shared with you that allow you to rethink your own. You've observed another person's work environment, attitudes, mood, even signs of their values. You've received feedback about your qualifications, experience, hopes, and dreams—if you asked for it. If you were especially wise, you've inquired not only about work and career but about life and balance, the role of career at various life stages, personal learning goals, community involvement, creative resources, and family and other relationships in connection to career decisions.

In our Focus Workshops we include a simple form for managing and tracking the information you acquire in informational/referral interviews. When you meet for the interview, you should take along this "contact sheet" and two copies of the current version of your Ah-ha résumé to use as a point of reference when you discuss your background and qualifications. In general, we don't advise our clients to send their résumé in advance unless the person you will be meeting with specifically requests it. This is not a job interview, and feedback about your résumé is only a part of what you should be seeking.

> **▪ So We Asked an Expert.**
> Kathleen Bullerman, Manager, Human Resources, Ameritech Cellular Services, says: "If we have no official position open and I meet someone who would be an excellent resource, I do whatever I can to find a slot for this person down the road. I target this individual and stay in touch. If someone goes on maternity leave or retires or moves, I'll call this person. I also pass the name on to others in the organization."
>
> **The Point:** Professional networking is part of every manager's job. So is finding good resources.

Focused Interview Contact Sheet

Contact name _____ Title _____

Business _____

Telephone _____ Fax _____

E-mail _____

Address _____

_____

Referral Source _____

Meeting Time _____ Meeting Date _____

Meeting Location _____

Meeting Objectives _____

_____

Specific Questions/Notes
1.

2.

3.

Additional Referrals from Contact (names, titles, addresses, phone numbers)
1.

2.

3.
Thank-you Note Sent _____

▪ AFTER THE INTERVIEW: STRATEGIC REVIEW ▪

Okay. You've had an informational/referral interview. Now what?

Now you will need to sort out and integrate what you've learned.
It will be up to you to select and use the information that helps you
gain further clarity. But you need to be the director, and you need to

retain your authority, even if you've just met someone who inspired you and whom you would like to imitate. Why do we add this word of caution? Because we know a little about human nature.

A doctor tells the story of a surgeon who greatly influenced him during his training. After several years in practice, he encountered his former teacher at a professional conference. "Dr. Snow," he said, "you were a wonderful mentor to me when I was in residency. I still use the techniques you taught me." He then described several specific surgeries and techniques. Dr. Snow replied, "Oh, my. I haven't used those techniques in years!"

Those who will be our strongest mentors, advisers, and advocates want nothing more than for us to continue to grow on our own beyond their inspiration. Forget that old saying about imitation being the sincerest form of flattery. Imitation isn't a form of flattery. In fact, at its most harmful, it reveals a lack of imagination and self-direction. Whatever you learn, take the time to refine it and develop it into your own.

As you pursue new career opportunities and directions, you should be integrating a strategy that includes assessing the opportunity that exists for you right now, analyzing your qualifications and history of achievement, constructing an ongoing network of the people you most need to meet, and beginning to meet with those people to add new knowledge to your overall vision. If this sounds like a lot of career *planning*, you may be surprised when we say it's also *career management*, and it's our recommendation for an ongoing plan. These activities support the ongoing development of Clarity, Strategy, and Action in relation to life and career growth.

▪ STRATEGIC EXPLORATIONS IN YOUR WORK SETTING ▪

Whether you are perfectly happy, moderately restless, or absolutely miserable in your current job, you owe it to yourself to scan the *local* horizon for opportunity. All right, if you're absolutely miserable, you might try scanning *new* horizons, but even in this case we'll encourage you to attempt a last-ditch strategy for healthy survival before bailing out. The current job market can swing from scarcity to abundance and back to scarcity again in just a few years. The burden of career stability and growth is on you, not on your company. Make it your responsibility, therefore, to create an action plan for your job (short-term goals to be achieved) and for your career (longer-term goals, planned by you and supported by others). There are two major benefits to doing so. First, you can make things happen: most organizations today recognize the value of a self-developing, self-appraising, self-motivated employee. Second, you can feel better about yourself, through your self-discovery and your actions.

Finding Challenges and Priorities in Your Workplace

As you seek better uses for your qualifications to do your best work, there are a few powerful directions you can take. In the last chapter we suggested that you identify people in your work setting who understand what's what and are aware of industry challenges, trends, and influences that will shape future opportunities. We encouraged you to find the decision-makers, resource-getters, and those who are regarded positively in your workplace.

You can use the interview protocols we've described or a less formal approach in your work setting once you've targeted the individuals you want to meet with. Your goal will be to articulate clearly your best-work qualifications and state plainly that you are open to the challenges your strengths can best address. The question then becomes, what are those challenges?

To prepare for internal interviews, you should review key documents such as the mission, vision, and strategic intent statements of your company. Look for statements of values and match them with your professional values. Ask yourself, "What is the relationship between my strengths and my company's priorities?"

Focus on specific departmental goals—yours and others'—that interest you. Think about the contributions you're currently making and those you could make to help meet these goals. Consider your job description, the one on paper in your personnel file. How have you already exceeded the requirements and expanded what you do on the job? What is the value you have added to your current position beyond what was expected when you were hired?

Determine the resources necessary to support and develop your future best work. What education, training, mentoring, or other opportunities do you need to grow your job, your career, and the company's success? (One company we know of has a policy that directs everyone wanting a promotion to identify and create a plan to mentor another into their current job before they are permitted to move up.)

Finally, remember the often forgotten rule of company-based career development: keep your progress tied to the vision of your organization. As one vice-president once said to us, "We aren't in the business of social services. I'm not interested in developing people. I'm interested in developing their skills for the company." Not everyone in authority will be so direct, but the bottom line is, literally, the bottom line. The good news is that most companies today will expect and encourage you to "look out for yourself" as long as you're also addressing the company's goals. The more those two merge, the better for everyone.

▪ THE JOB INTERVIEW: A MUTUAL EXPLORATION ▪

As you may have noticed, we are attempting to help you build an integrated strategy to understand the best work of your life and then go after it. In particular, we are offering a layered approach for building a strategy that includes identifying and initiating opportunities toward that best-work goal.

Naturally, such opportunities include job interviews. But we aren't going to launch into a "make 'em want you bad" discussion about cunning job interview techniques. The truth is, if and when you have a job interview, the most important thing to remember is that the interview is a mutual exploration. Although everybody talks about job *hunting*, you should not be trying to stalk, ambush, and capture a job any more than the interviewers should be trying to throw a net over you. (If they are, be very careful.)

The point of a job interview is to find out if a match can be made

So We Asked an Expert: Rebecca Chekouras, relates: "You can learn a lot about a company that interests you in advance of an interview. It's not simply an advantage to be 'in the know' for an interview, it's an expectation in the information age."

The Point: Get informed and excited about the company —before the interview.

between a company's needs and your willingness and ability to fulfill them. First, let's focus on preparation for the job interview.

Preparing for an Interview

Have you done your homework? What do you know about the company or organization? Have you used the library, Internet, and business publications to learn about the company? Have you called, stopped by, or written to the company to gather available print materials? Most organizations have annual reports, special publications, brochures, and newsletters. Even the smallest workplace usually has a public relations or marketing strategy to help others learn about their products or services. The people in the human resources department may be willing to send you internal documents if they are relevant to the "work culture," once they know you are scheduled to interview with their company. Try to learn everything you can—not so that you can dazzle the interviewers with what you've learned, but so you can integrate the information into your overall strategy.

Ask yourself the following questions. Does the company's mission excite and interest me? Does the style seem compatible with mine? Is the size of the company, the location, and what I've learned about the company's internal culture appealing? Compare, for example, an organization serving the homeless and one that offers long-distance hauling. Your qualifications may be useful to either, but the "feeling" inside will be vastly different. Think hard about your preferences.

Once you've researched the company in relation to your needs, values, and preferences, think about the job itself. Whether the position is in sales and marketing, in research and development, in a communications department, or in a technical division, you can research it to understand industry standards and practices. You can call on professional and trade organizations to help you discover state-of-the-art functions in different types of industries.

This is homework you can and should do. If you're attempting to transfer your skills to a new industry, you'll find it particularly fascinating and valuable to learn about the current best practices and the latest challenges and trends in your area of expertise, but with a new slant. Create an informed picture of your strengths in the new setting, and your job interview preparation will take on added depth. Remember: you aren't trying to get "all the answers" to pretend to be smarter than you are. In fact, answers may be less important than questions. If you come up with focused questions as a result of your research, you'll probably score a few points with interviewers. And you'll get valuable insights from them as a result of your curiosity.

Making Your Move

Study the job description or listing and analyze the requirements. How strong a match can you make with your qualifications? You'll probably be asked to send in a résumé along with your job application and cover letter. It's important to consider the type of résumé you will send. Your Ah-ha résumé will provide a strong resource of content choices.

You may be thinking, "But I haven't finished my Ah-ha résumé yet!" Don't worry about it. Read the last line of the previous paragraph once again: Your Ah-ha résumé will provide a strong resource of content choices. That means that you take what's in it and use it as you need to. A completed résumé may do many people more harm than good, because they may treat it as if it were etched in stone and try to use it as is for every job situation. Your Ah-ha résumé is *you*: be flexible with it, shape it, rearrange it, and present it according to the occasion.

Large companies hiring for entry-level positions often use résumé scanning software, so you want to make sure to include appropriate keywords indicated in their job description or list of requirements. Many executives tell us that they have only one or two minutes to scan a résumé before deciding which to keep and which to set aside. If you're entering a highly competitive application process and want to make sure you aren't eliminated on your choice of résumé format, try to find out which format is preferred. Small businesses or those hiring at the executive level frequently prefer an emphasis on skills rather than a chronological listing of work history. We've even seen attractive résumés at executive levels that were made up only of a bullet-pointed list of major achievement results.

You'll need to determine the best format for the company you're approaching. There are several dozen books out there in your library or local bookstores showing hundreds of résumé formats. Choose one you think will be suited to the company you are approaching.

But don't create a new résumé without drawing directly from your Ah-ha résumé. Why would you even consider doing such a thing? You've done the careful work of identifying, analyzing, and articulating your best work. Use it as a bank of valuable resources to fashion more conventional "official" résumés that are sometimes required.

If you need to rephrase your qualifications to fit the job description requirements, do so. If you choose to remove skills and strengths that seem irrelevant to the specific position, you may. But you wouldn't be heading into an interview if there weren't significant interest on both parts—that is, if you and a potential employer didn't believe there was a possible fit between the position and your skills and strengths—so make sure to state your qualifications strongly and clearly.

If the organization doesn't require a business, technologically formatted, or specific résumé style, your Ah-ha résumé, carefully edited and tailored to the job opportunity, will be a perfectly appropriate one to send.

Finally, consider what generally comes first on a résumé—your objective. When you shape your résumé for a specific position, study and tailor the objective to fit the job description in a truthful manner. Go from general to specific, according to what you know about the position, the company, and the industry. A few examples:

· Seeking opportunity to apply project management skills to needs of a rapidly growing publishing company.
· Seeking opportunity to utilize strategic communication skills to leverage awareness of new community programs.
· Seeking opportunity to apply key qualifications—sensitive communication, high level of productivity, and rapid learning capacity—in agency serving public education systems.

As we noted above, the interview is a mutual exploration of a possible fit between your qualifications and the company's needs. You should tailor the objective of your Ah-ha résumé to reflect your intention for meeting with the interviewers. If you aren't comfortable being so specific, be general, but make sure your objective and their needs have some overlap.

What about not including the objective? It's up to you, so feel free to omit it from your résumé. Your cover letter, your appearance, and what you say at the interview are also strong statements of your objective.

▪ THE AH-HA RÉSUMÉ AS PRIMARY RESOURCE ▪

Use your Ah-ha résumé to prepare in every way possible. It is the workhorse in your stable of resources. In other words, it's not just useful when you're taking the first step in applying for a job. It's a tool to help you make the most of any interview opportunity.

So We Asked an Expert. Pam Wegner, Vice-President, Information Technology and Administration, Wisconsin Power and Light, explains: "I react positively to a résumé that doesn't look like a form but shows that the person has spent some time trying to find out my problems and how their skills will help solve them."

The Point: That's the purpose of your Ah-ha résumé.

As soon as a prospective employer calls to schedule an interview, pull out your Ah-ha résumé and start preparing. It's not enough just to show up. Part of every good strategy is preparation.

You've outlined certain strengths and skills in your application. The interviewer will naturally want to focus on those qualifications. So practice talking about your relevant strengths and skills with a friend or colleague until it sounds completely natural for you to describe your qualifications. Most people have some difficulty "blowing their own horn"—a phrase that our clients often use to express a common concern. If you must, you can admit during the interview that you usually don't do such things. The interview provides an acceptable opportunity to promote yourself, so by all means do so. Practice will help.

Again, your achievements will provide the narrative you need to maintain control of your part of the interview. Prepare carefully by studying your stories and being able to pull significant items from each achievement. Then, during the interview, use the Ah-ha résumé as a point of reference, directing the interviewer to the achievement you're referring to. Most human resource professionals rely on "behavioral" interviews that explore past behaviors as predictors of future success. Your Ah-ha résumé is a treasure trove of your best behaviors and the results they created; continue to use it as a focal point during the interview.

The education and training section of your résumé should be a source of pride to you. If the discussion turns to growth opportunities, be ready to use this section to point out continuous learning and your desire to develop knowledge and skills in a new position. Ask about the company's policies and resources concerning professional development. Remember: you're interviewing the company, too.

The remaining sections of your Ah-ha résumé may repeat much of what is listed on a chronological one. But if you have additional items, such as volunteer work, awards, special nonwork projects, refer to them and always bring the stories and experiences back to a focus on your key qualifications. You want to be remembered as the one "who had such a strong combination of people skills and financial management" or the one "who certainly has some good insights about her strengths."

Again and again, our clients have told of interviewers who say, "You really seem to know yourself!" after an interview in which they used their Ah-ha résumé as a resource. So make sure you bring a copy as a kind of script to use during the interview to remind you of your strengths and accomplishments.

Attitude

Although we've repeatedly stressed enthusiasm and positive human relations throughout the book, a word to the wise is due again. Everyone we talk to stresses these as the most important requirements for any job: *enthusiasm* and *positive human relations*. No one willingly hires a person who is emotionally flat or who lacks people skills. Your version of these characteristics may be subdued or expressive, but enthusiasm and positive human relations *must* be evident. Part of your preparation will be to underscore these factors in your previous accomplishments. By being confident about what you've done and what you can and want to do, your enthusiasm is naturally bolstered and will come across in the interview. What can hinder enthusiasm is uncertainty about what you can do and what you're looking for, and you can be sure this will come across in an interview just as well.

We hope it goes without saying that preparation for a job interview is not about trying to anticipate "trick" questions or trying to find "the right approach." There are books available on dressing for success, anticipating the hundred most frequently asked questions, creating military-like strategies to "capture the enemy," and so on. If you want to pursue these approaches, we encourage you to browse the libraries and bookstores. Dressing for success, for example, is important: dressing appropriately is key not only to making a good impression but also to making you comfortable enough to avoid distraction. But the right approach, if you truly want to direct and manage your career, is to spend your time preparing to explore a match between the company and you. The goal of the interview is to obtain a job offer. But the offer must be one you really want because it will allow you to do your best work.

▪ FINALLY, ABOUT DESPERATION ▪

We aren't heartless. We know what it feels like to need a job and to want a job so badly that almost anything will do. We've experienced the temptation to change shape, to fit in, just to get over the misery of joblessness or to escape an intolerable job. But there's something more important that we know: taking a job out of desperation is not the answer. People seeking career help tell us all the time about what it feels like to aimlessly move forward, or to be emotionally paralyzed, or to be angry all the time, pulled in a direction not of their choosing, trapped in mediocre work—when all they wanted was to do their best. The price of compromise is high.

If you're wrestling with issues of compromise, the Me/Now spot on your Lifeline is the place to stand. Understand that a job that is uninspiring, a poor fit, a mediocre opportunity, an unhealthful work environment, will probably last for two, five, maybe ten years. Mark your Lifeline with that realization. Do you want to spend that amount of your life doing something you don't like? Try to find a way to support your strategic career development. Use a temp agency or find freelance work. Or stay in your unsatisfactory job long enough to support a strategic career search. Consider the hours you spend on your career plan to be your primary job until you find your best work. You should be using your insights to create connections, explore opportunities, and initiate contacts. You're already on your way!

▪ CONTINUING EVOLUTION OF YOUR AH-HA RÉSUMÉ ▪

As you go through the interview process and meet with various people, you will learn what makes a difference to them as well as how your strengths, skills, and preferences can meet their needs. Use what you learn to refine your Ah-ha résumé. Here is what we mean:

Objective. Tailor to specific opportunities.

Qualifications. Refine language in relation to the needs of industries and companies you're exploring.

Achievements. Continue to refine and tighten descriptions. Select achievements based on specific interview settings. Spend time practicing talking about achievements, results, best-work examples. Get conversational and comfortable with all your "stories" of best work.

Employment and Related Experience. Refine for most powerful listing. Determine whether to keep or temporarily delete items not related to specific opportunities.

Education and Training. Add any additional professional development you've overlooked. Use this section as a platform to discuss professional development in the future in all interview settings.

Awards and Honors. Select awards and honors tailored to specific interview opportunities. Get feedback in informational settings about content you've included in this section.

ACTION STEPS FOR MAPPING AND TRACKING OPPORTUNITY

1. Identify two or three people you want to meet with for information and/or referrals in relation to career growth and development. Following the protocols described in this chapter, create a schedule of appointments with strategic learning goals. Do all

follow-up activities described—post-interview analysis, strategy refinement, thank-you note to interviewer.

2. Create next steps to further refine your knowledge or to act on opportunities presented through previous interviews.

3. Begin to practice speaking about your best work using your Ah-ha résumé as a script. Work with a friend or professional colleague and solicit feedback for further improvements.

4. Continue to use your Lifeline for perspective and your LifeCircle for resource development. Schedule time to work on career development and use a system of action steps and goals to meet. Keep the goals at an achievable level. When you've met two or three goals, review your strategy and then refine and set additional goals.

5. Assess your current job setting for possible expanded opportunities. If you're open to jobs outside of your current setting, let others know (discreetly). The next chapter will describe strategic approaches to initiating best-work opportunities and will include an effective cover letter for specific job applications.

nine

Initiating Appropriate Strategies

One Monday afternoon Darlene Goodfit was pulled, barely breathing, from beneath a pile of letters, many of them attached to heavy résumés. Officials at the Uneedus Corporation did not return calls after word leaked out that Ms. Goodfit, the human resource manager, had attempted to take her life by diving into the mound of paper rather than reading the letters.

Reached at City Hospital later that day, Ms. Goodfit said, "I just can't win! We've had over four hundred responses to our classified ad for a middle manager. They all look alike and sound alike. I don't know who would fit our needs. I guess I just became mesmerized—I was trying to sort them, then I blanked out. That's all I remember."

The exhausted and somewhat shaken manager took an indefinite leave of absence. Meanwhile, Uneedus issued a request that the public refrain from sending further applications.

▪ THE REALITY ▪

In the last two chapters we've concentrated on *understanding and building* a strategy to identify and uncover opportunities for new work. Now it's time for you to *initiate* a strategy in order to move your career development along.

If you've identified opportunities you'd like to pursue, let's make sure you do so effectively. If you haven't yet focused on specific, targeted goals, the tools and tactics in the following pages will help you get ready to take the initiative once you have a direction in mind.

Whatever your status at this point, when you're ready to apply for positions, you'll want to do what you can to prevent flooding human resource offices with unfocused hopes out of desperation. After all, those who receive your application want what you want: they want to find the right match for their job openings. And you can help them once you understand their needs.

You may be ready to seek referrals and information from several networks. You may be ready to create a new project or direction for your work in a current job setting. You may be ready to leave your current job, but still feel willing to try a last-ditch approach to revitalize opportunity there. You may be ready to write a proposal to do work in an entirely new setting, one that isn't even advertising a position. In all of these cases there are ways to initiate opportunity—if you understand the view from the other side of the desk and make an appropriate approach.

▪ TWO NECESSITIES: ORGANIZATION AND DREAM HOUSES ▪

Now that you've become committed to increasing your clarity about your best work and because you'll need to invest time for focused research to identify marketplace opportunity, you'll need to map out your explorations in some detail. Navigating the map will mean using your time carefully and maintaining a healthy level of motivation. You need to get organized, and you need to stay powerful.

If you're already a time-management wizard, congratulations! When we work with clients, we're sometimes amazed by how cleverly people manage their complex lives. Other clients confound us by stating simply, "Oh. I forgot my résumé." Or "Were we supposed to meet last week?" Having and keeping a detailed calendar to maintain control over your career activity isn't an *option;* it's a *requirement.*

There are a variety of time-management systems on the market you can explore through libraries and bookstores. A simple way to shop for a system is to go to one of those office supply superstores and wander into the business calendar section. You'll find lots of appointment books with a myriad of options for organizing your time (and your life). Study them carefully to see which system appeals to you. Many of the publishers who offer such systems provide numbers you can call to learn about their company's time-management training. You can attend a training session, send for audiotapes, or purchase detailed books about the company's time-management philosophy. Some of these systems provide approaches thorough enough to include explorations of values and lifestyle issues.

Choose a system, take the time to understand it, and apply it to your life and career. If you're thinking, "I'm not the type of person who needs/can use a formal system," understand that you'll have a hard time keeping track of the amount of information that flows once you begin your career initiatives. And you'll risk being unprofessional when things slip up. If those time-management systems seem too much, you can certainly use a simple, inexpensive pocket calendar. What matters is not the type of system you choose, but that you use it.

Keeping an organized calendar of career-related activities—meetings, correspondence, names, addresses (regular and e-mail), phone and fax numbers—will help you feel in control and enable you to see the resources you're building. You'll be managing many levels of unrelated activity, and it will be impossible to do this without a good system. Which brings us to our second, and related, thought: selecting two dream houses.

We're predicting that you'll have lots to keep track of because we recommend creating more than one initiative at a time. We call this strategy for feeling more powerful and less vulnerable "falling in love with two dream houses." If you've ever purchased a house, you know that the best way to get your dream house is to become interested in two houses. When you begin negotiations for the first, you'll be better able to state your terms, explore options, and consider making an offer if you have another house in mind as well. If you have only one option, you'll be more inclined to compromise, to grasp at the only available opportunity.

We worry about clients who are pursuing a great idea and are so single-minded that they become overly invested in one career possibility to the exclusion of others. As one opportunity heats up, it's tempting to put others on the back burner. Yet that's exactly the time to keep other options equally active, even to press forward.

For example, you might be interviewing for a position in a large corporation while exploring (through informational interviews) a new start-up company in your community. Your skills would be equally valuable in each setting. Each offers a unique and attractive possibility for your best work, and you can envision success either way. The corporate position would be a good fit, but you have one or two reservations about reentering the mainstream full throttle. The start-up company isn't actively recruiting, but you've learned from your informational interviews that it's rapidly growing and currently contracting with independent professionals.

"Contingency" employment is the way many permanent employees get started. Now is the time to press for both opportunities. By pursuing both possibilities enthusiastically, you'll be forced to look more closely at each, to ask for more detailed information, and to present a proposal or consider an offer more clearly. If one of the opportunities doesn't pan out, you have the other to pursue. The best outcome, of course, will be to secure both options and enjoy the choice of a buyer's market.

▪ INITIATING ACTIVITY: GETTING "ALL OVER THE MAP" ▪

We'll now presume that you're organized and motivated to commit time, preferably structured and nonnegotiable time, to your career development. Before we get too far into the tools and tactics for making things happen, study the Interviewing for Impact Map. The three types of interviews—referral, informational, and job—that we introduced in Chapter 8 illustrate the various levels of activity that will occupy some of your time.

INTERVIEWING FOR IMPACT: A THREE-PHASE MAP

IF I AM . . .	UNFOCUSED	GETTING FOCUSED	VERY FOCUSED
Plan for a . . .	· Referral interview	· Informational interview	· Job or work-related interview
Meet with . . .	· People who know a lot of people—friends, acquaintances, lawyers, doctors, dentists, clergy, etc.	· People who know "what's what" within specific careers, companies, professions, industries	· People who are decision-makers or those with influence in identifying and hiring for human resources
Plan agenda to include . . .	· Key qualifications and interest in career exploration · Discussion of possible directions · Names of others to talk to	· Discussion of career exploration and key qualifications · Information and advice from his/her personal experience · Key insights about trends, needs for specific resources · Names of others to talk to	· Presentation of qualifications as a match for requirements of company · Discussion of previous achievements and results · Clarification of opportunity for a match: job, project specifics · Next steps
Aim for results . . .	· Feedback about qualifications, current directions · Referrals, contacts · Advocacy, ongoing interest in your progress	· Information about companies to explore · Feedback to refine your thinking, tailor qualifications · Referrals · Advocacy	· Job, work possibilities · Information for next-phase interview · Framework for proposal for work
Follow up with . . .	· Thank-you note, including your intentions to use his/her name for referrals · Promise to keep him/her informed of progress	· Thank-you note with specific references to his/her key points, advice, etc. · Promise to keep him/her informed of progress	· Thank-you note with direct statement of interest, enthusiasm · Promise to call for information on decision or for next steps in interview process

Follow up with . . . *(Cont)*	· Progress note after you've met with referrals	· Progress notes as referral interviews occur, with key insights gained in each	· Send second note if time passes and no contact has been made
Tools, tactics . . .	· Ah-ha résumé and ability to discuss it conversationally	· Ah-ha résumé as script for presenting qualifications, discussion of achievements	· Cover letter matching your qualifications with job requirements exactly · Résumé tailored to company style, preferences · Ah-ha résumé as additional resource to expand discussion
Ah-ha résumé evolution . . .	· Still a work in progress	· Somewhat tailored. Use as script for brainstorming, getting advice	· Refined, polished, tailored, to specific opportunity

If you're unfocused but curious about a new direction, you'll meet with people who can provide referrals to help you find those "in the know" who can satisfy your curiosities. Once you've found them, you'll move into an informational interview phase until you identify specific work or job opportunities. We call this "getting focused." When you're ready to try for a position or to initiate work opportunity, you'll feel very focused. Meanwhile, we hope you will continue the cycle as you explore additional options. This means that you might be very focused in one area of exploration but only beginning to learn about another. The map is designed to help you track your progress and analyze your activity to keep moving on an upward trajectory toward the goal of getting the best work of your life. Use it as a checkpoint. And remember: interviewing is also a good tool for exploring internal options within your company, and it works well if you've decided to seek the perfect "serious volunteer" activity in the community to broaden your networks. The suggestions on the map will be appropriate for exploring best-work opportunities in your career and in the other areas of your LifeCircle.

▪ PRACTICAL TOOLS FOR INITIATING OPPORTUNITIES ▪

Review our discussions in Chapter 8 about approaching people you want to meet in a courteous and personal manner. It's important to explain your purpose and to communicate how their specific knowledge is important to you. You must also make it easier for them to help you efficiently by making a request for a brief meeting, one that will guarantee a positive outcome. The meeting should allow you to meet your specific expectations and objectives successfully. The people you contact will want to feel they helped in some way. If they come up with additional ideas or resources for you, it will be because they feel a sense of advocacy, because they feel they've helped simply by meeting with you.

▪ REFERRAL INTERVIEWS ▪

Objectives

If you're requesting a meeting to gain referrals, your objectives, as our map suggests, will be to make a positive connection, get feedback about goals, and acquire the names of two or three people you can talk to. If the meeting is positive and the person you meet with seems invested in helping make things happen for you, he or she may even give you additional career-related ideas.

Initiating Contact

Whether you telephone or write a note when seeking referrals, it's wise to include these points. These are just suggestions: be sure to use words that sound like you.

· I'm calling you because you are knowledgeable about the community (company, our industry, etc.).
· I'm currently exploring professional options in a systematic way in order to learn more about the ways I might work in the future.
· One of the areas that has caught my interest is _____, and I'm hoping to meet one or two people connected with that industry (department, project, etc.) to learn more.

· I'd like to get together at your convenience for a brief meeting to describe my career explorations and ask your help in brainstorming with me based on your perspective.

If you're calling, set up a time to get together during the call. If you're writing a note, say when you'll call to make an appointment.

▪ INFORMATIONAL INTERVIEWS ▪

Objectives

Before you write or call to ask for an appointment for an informational interview, review your strategy and focus on the best possible objectives to set for a meeting with this person. Find out all you can about his or her expertise and general knowledge. Consider the types of questions you will ask that will maximize your time with him or her. Again, these questions should make the most of your contact with that person. You should have already gotten as much information from other sources as possible.

Concerning work-related issues, ask about:

· Career path
· Decisions in career development
· Choice of industry
· Specific advice about your decisions
· Feedback about your qualifications
· Application of your skills in his or her field
· Work environment, atmosphere
· Visions he or she has for work
· Work-related community involvement
· Continuing learning habits
· Best day at work
· Worst day at work

Concerning life-related issues, ask about:

· Keeping balance
· Integrating values into decisions and career choices
· Selection of geographic location
· Personal growth in the midst of career
· Visions for his or her future
· Community identity
· Creative outlets
· Setting family and individual goals

And always:

· Focus on what you want to learn.
· Underscore the reasons why his or her input is important to you.
· Ask advice on next steps in your exploration.
· Seek the names of additional people to meet with and secure permission to use his or her name as a referral.

Initiating Contact

So We Asked an Expert. Pam Wegner, Vice-President, Information Technology and Administration, Wisconsin Power and Light, states: "I have recently started giving informational interviews. I find that they are very helpful. They are freeing for me because I don't have to give a job to someone, I just have to give information."

The Point: You will feel free, too, if you are seeking information about a possible career and not secretly hoping for a job offer.

Again, you may call, write, or e-mail the person you want to meet. Bear in mind that these will be busy people, and an approach that offers them lead time and discretion in scheduling an appointment will be important. Your communication may be intercepted by a secretary or voice mail, so be prepared to state succinctly the source of the referral and the reasons you are seeking a brief time to meet with the person you've selected. Clearly state that you're not asking for a job opportunity but exploring career directions in a strategic way by gaining important insights from people who have been highly recommended.

Suggestions for phrasing:

· _____ (referral source) recently suggested that I get in touch with you. I am currently exploring some new directions for my future, and he/she thought you would be of particular help because of your expertise in (interest in, knowledge about, experience with) _____ (company, industry).
· I would especially appreciate your insights about _____ (specifics in relation to his/her position).
· I'd like to request a chance to get together at your convenience for a very brief meeting, ten or fifteen minutes. I'm preparing a few key questions about _____ (his or her personal insights regarding your objectives).

If this approach is a letter, e-mail, or voice mail, say:

· I'll call your office early next week to schedule an appointment. (Specifying the time will allow the person to okay an appointment with a secretary or to talk with you directly when the secretary announces your call.)

If this is a phone call and you are speaking with the person you want to meet:

· Be sure to stress the reasons you want to meet him or her in particular.
· Emphasize that you will be brief and available to meet at his or her convenience.
· Don't mention a résumé unless he or she requests one. Your Ah-ha résumé will provide a script for part of your meeting, but should not be the focal point.

▪ JOB INTERVIEWS ▪

Objectives

As you prepare to respond to a job listing or a classified ad, the view from the other side of the desk is critically important. Do you remember the plight of Darlene Goodfit, described at the start of this chapter? The description of the deluge of applications that overwhelmed her should make you aware of what employers face. Executives and other decision-makers are charged with the continuous responsibility of sorting through information. Their first instinct is generally to get rid of anything that seems useless to them or too confusing to be worthy of their time. Sometimes résumés fall in this category.

Most busy executives become adept at making rapid decisions about their incoming mail, faxes, e-mails, and phone messages. Imagine yourself sitting at a desk piled dangerously high with such information, as well as memos, articles, and reports. You turn to the incoming pile. The phone rings throughout the process. The recycling bin is nearby. Talk . . . sort . . . toss . . . talk . . . sort . . . toss . . . Much of what comes into your office goes out with the custodian. A few pieces of mail survive because you consider them relevant to the company's needs, interesting, or just deserving of at least another glance. Every piece of mail you don't toss means follow-up action, communication, and additional work. Something in each piece that you keep shows promise of value.

When your company advertises a job opening and you're part of the screening and/or hiring committee, your desk is further burdened with letters and résumés representing additional sorting and decision-making stretching out for days, even weeks. You face a formidable challenge: you must find the five or ten candidates most suitable for an interview, most likely to be of value to the company. It isn't unusual to see executives on airplanes, in airport lounges, or on their way to their cars lugging batches of résumés to be sorted and judged. Whenever you end up with the pile of paper, you have a paradoxical task. The brain commands, "Find the good ones and do it fast." Then the brain quickly adds, "Start by getting rid of the bad ones. And do that even faster."

So, to choose the best possible candidates efficiently, you first must eliminate all those you can. You look for reasons to do so. "No direct sales experience." "Nothing much about communication skills." "Pretty lackluster work history." "Just starting out." Over and over you find flaws, perceive mismatches, get a gut feeling that frees you to reject an application in order to reduce the pile, to identify the few applications worthy of an interview.

Now, for just another moment, stay in the role of the recipient of those applications. Imagine finding an application that establishes relevance and value at first glance. A succinct cover letter, a tailored résumé that you simply must put in the "short pile." What would it look like? What would it say?

Okay, now switch roles again. You're back to applying for a position. Your objective in seeking an interview must be to create an immediately obvious match between the company's needs and your qualifications. You must move beyond the role of applicant and get into the role of directing the information. You must present the recipient of your application with the potential benefits of meeting with you in a way that brings him or her relief from the burden of reviewing and sorting. The response you want is "Here's a good candidate. We can't afford not to interview this one."

Naturally, you should strongly believe in the possibility of a match. Otherwise, we hope you wouldn't be applying. Remember: your goal is not just to get a job, but to get an opportunity to do your best work. To make sure you've selected an appropriate opportunity, we recommend a detailed analysis of the job listing and a perfectly tailored cover letter.

So We Asked an Expert. Marcia Koslov, Wisconsin State Law Librarian, notes: "The cover letter, even more than the résumé, indicates suitability for the job. Those that stand out are the ones that demonstrate immediately a strong match with our requirements."

The Point: Those who review résumés and cover letters need a reason to keep yours in the short stack.

Initiating Contact

Begin by thoroughly reviewing the job listing or classified ad. List each requirement exactly as it's described. Read the description again for "hidden requirements"—expectations, assumptions, and so forth that you might miss at first or dismiss as inconsequential. Remember: if it's in the ad, assume that it's there for a reason. Add those requirements to the list in the order in which they appear.

Here's an example to show what we mean:

Uneedus Corporation placed an ad in the *New York Times* for a project director. In the text of the classified ad that follows, we've marked all the requirements with italics.

> ***Project Director.*** Uneedus, a leading international management and consulting firm, seeks *highly skilled, innovative* management professional. The *dynamic* Project Director we seek will *lead an interdisciplinary team* implementing a *highly successful*, multicountry-funded health project.
>
> *Strategic planning, client orientation,* and *diplomatic skills* essential. The new director will have at least *five years senior management experience* and the *proven ability to manage complex projects, multicultural personnel,* and *financial resources. Commitment to advancing preventive health education programs* is a must. Candidates must hold an *applicable advanced degree* and have a *sense of humor.*
>
> The position is *located in the Washington, D.C. metro area and* will require at least *25% international travel, some of it arduous.*

Now think of a succinct but powerful description of your experience or qualifications that matches each requirement. Remember: you're trying to help the executive get through the mail by allowing her or him to say "Yes!" to your letter. The strongest candidates will be the ones who meet or surpass every requirement and who capture the spirit of that position because they feel it will allow them to do the best work of their lives.

"Perfect Match" Letter

Use a standard business format with headings and correct titles of company contacts. Then begin the text of your letter with a statement (in your own style) that essentially says:

> *I am writing in response to your listing for the Project Director position that appeared in the March 17th edition of the* New York Times. *The scope of responsibility described forms a perfect match with my qualifications. The challenges implied in this exciting position mirror my experience and my commitment to the field of preventive health care and an expanding global influence of companies like Uneedus. I have taken the liberty to match my qualifications to the requirements you have listed in the advertisement.*

List the requirements in the order in which they appear in the advertisement. Create a parallel list of your qualifications with a very strong but brief statement of achievement.

YOUR REQUIREMENTS:	MY QUALIFICATIONS:
Highly skilled, innovative manager	Twelve years of experience in assessment and creation of community health initiatives in the rural South.
Dynamic Project Director	Annual increases in service in all past programs through community advocacy and revenue diversification.
Lead interdisciplinary team	Managed health care and education professionals in successful collaborations for five years.
Strategic planning	Continuing education credentials in strategic planning. Formal plans completed, implemented during past two years.
Client orientation	Five years direct-service delivery to clients. Seven years supervision of direct services.

Diplomatic skills	Proven expertise in positive shared-outcome negotiations in complex political environment in past program director position.
Five years senior management experience	Seven years senior management experience.
Proven ability to manage complex projects	Past five years managed multiple projects serving three population segments with accountability to five revenue sources.
Manage multicultural personnel	Training in cultural diversity and successful recruitment and training of fully integrated staff. Retention rate 90% over five years.
Manage financial resources	Seven years experience in managing budget of over one million dollars.
Commitment to preventive programs	Published article on the importance of prevention for measurable outcomes, *Health News* magazine, May 1995. Twelve-year career in prevention agencies and organizations.
Advanced degree	M.S. Social Work, University of Virginia. Continuing education in all aspects of community health programming, 1987–present.
Sense of humor	Commitment to quality-of-life environment in work setting, including balance, humor, support, and celebration.
Washington, D.C., location	Willing to relocate immediately.
Arduous international travel	Resilient, fitness-oriented, eager traveler.

In this example, we've used an ad that contains plenty of requirements to give you a good idea of what's possible in creating a match. Notice that the cover letter is not just a formality to accompany your résumé. The purpose of the letter is to demonstrate an enthusiastic match, to save the reader from having to search through your résumé to find the appropriate qualifications. Your résumé will simply underscore and provide a framework for the perfect-match letter.

What if you're very interested in a position but you're not a *perfect* match? If there are one or two requirements you simply don't meet, but you're very enthusiastic and certain you could fill the position, try to list an "equivalency." If the ad specifies a master's degree and you don't have one, you might try stating, "Ten years of experience equivalent to advanced degree credential." If the ad calls for proficiency in specified software applications and you don't have that proficiency, you can say, "Willingness to acquire software application training at my expense." Again, the reason to build a strong case and to identify equivalencies is if (and only if) you've found an exciting opportunity, and you're very eager to explore a match.

▪ AFTER THE INTERVIEW ▪

Okay, now we'll jump ahead a little. Somebody from the company contacts you to schedule an interview. You meet with the interviewer(s), and you make the most of the opportunity to show why you feel there's a suitable fit between your qualifications and the requirements for the position. Then what?

If you develop and use the strategies we discussed in Chapter 8, the interview will reveal whether or not there is a mutual sense of opportunity. Take time to sort out your reactions and identify additional questions. It's almost always impossible to tell what the interviewers are thinking at the time of the interview because they must keep an open mind throughout their meeting with you and with others. They will not reach a decision until all interviews have been completed. During the interview, you should be able to ask about the timeline for the interviewing process and the target date for filling the position. This will give you a sense of when you might hear back from the interviewers.

Follow-up Letters

Write a brief thank-you note immediately after the interview. This can be a very simple matter. Again, be sure to use words that sound like you. The first and last paragraphs are basic. You may also want to add a detail or two, as shown here in the middle paragraph, to help

them remember you and to remind them of any particular strengths
that you demonstrated during your meeting.

> *Thank you for taking the time to meet with me today to discuss
> the position of marketing director. The responsibilities sound chal-
> lenging and exciting.*
>
> *I was particularly impressed when Ms. Anderson talked about
> how the marketing director would work with the people in research
> and development and in customer service to ensure more effective
> promotional efforts. That is the method I advocated when I worked
> as a marketing project manager, because I believe that collaboration
> is essential among people who are developing and selling any product
> or service.*
>
> *I would like to express again my interest in the position and my
> hope that you will find me most qualified to join the team at (com-
> pany name).*

That's it: simply a few words to thank the people who interviewed you
and to show that you're still interested in the position.

Later, if the deadline passes for filling the position and you haven't
heard from the company, it's appropriate to write a note to restate your
interest. If you want the position, say so. Don't assume a decision has
been made simply because the date has passed. Hiring processes get
sidetracked regularly. In addition, there may be two or three top con-
tenders for the job, and the company may need to schedule another
round of interviews. You will want to stay in the loop.

A friend of ours who owns her own company told us that she is
grateful for a follow-up thank-you letter from job applicants who have
not been selected. She wants to keep them in her resource pool for
future consideration and needs to know that they liked the company
and remain interested. She has even contacted and hired such people
as future jobs opened up.

Letters to "Rekindle the Romance"

Once you've gone to the trouble of researching, approaching, and
interviewing with a company, consider that you have established a
relationship. When and if you are pursuing future opportunities with

a company, always stay in touch and let the contact(s) you've made there know of your positive regard.

One of our clients relates the following benefits of keeping in touch.

> *Early in my career I missed being hired for a position but was told I was "first runner-up." I was curious about the woman they had selected and how she would do in her new job. Not long after the interviews, I introduced myself to her at a professional gathering, and she was happy to know of our mutual connection. Over the years we became good friends and have generously helped each other with our careers.*

ଌ ଌ ଌ

▪ CURRENT WORKPLACE OPPORTUNITIES ▪

Objectives

Throughout this book we've encouraged you to grow and reach for your best work even in current settings that are less than ideal. There are many advantages to remaining in a setting where you've established a work history: you're familiar with the organization, you have friendships and concrete benefits. By reclarifying your goals and values, skills, preferences, and strengths, you may, indeed, begin to have a sense of possibility in this company you might not have imagined.

If so, you can use all the strategies, tools, and tactics we've described so far and adapt them to your setting. It will be important to invest time to research opportunity in the ways we've suggested in Chapters 7 and 8. Once you have a sense of new opportunity in your current organization, you can consider writing a proposal to expand, redefine, or change your current job. Your Ah-ha résumé will be, as always, a key resource. Most decision-makers in any setting will need to be reminded of successful behaviors from the past. Your analysis of your accomplishments will strengthen your case for future challenges and remind the person you meet with of projects possibly long forgotten. As always, you must know what you want to offer and find out where and why your offer will be of most value. That is called *finding your best work*.

White Paper Proposal

A white paper proposal is a brief description of a need you've identified in the organization and a plan you're proposing to address the need. A key task in such a proposal is to offer information in a way that's highly motivational. Imagine, again, being the person who receives such a document. If you were to receive a white paper proposal from someone in your company asking for an opportunity to change the way he or she worked, what would you need to know?

· Statement of the problem or challenge you want to address, with facts and figures to document it as a priority
· Description of skills and proven strengths the writer of the proposal offers as a resource
· Suggestions of possible ways the work could progress
· Explanation of how his or her current work would get accomplished in the meantime
· Suggestion for a time and date to meet to discuss further

So We Asked an Expert: Peg Davey, Staff Associate, Office of the Provost, Coordinator of Student Orientation, Advising, and Registration, University of Wisconsin–Madison, explains: "When I needed a change, I took a long look at the changing needs around me. I've been in administration for a very long time, and I knew I could offer high-level skills and flexibility wherever needed. I created a proposal based on a strategy to 'plug in' resources in valuable ways. My career is completely revitalized."

The Point: Your current workplace may provide a whole new career.

An important thing to remember when initiating such an innovation is that the person you approach may not be the sole decision-maker in such matters. He or she may have to act as an advocate for your proposal to the others it will affect. You can help that happen. Your document needs to be simple enough that he or she can explain it briefly but clearly and point out the key ideas, benefits, and steps you've suggested for implementation of your ideas. If you do this well, it will be hard to ignore, especially if you have correctly pinpointed a need and have a sound approach for dealing with that need.

Last-Ditch Proposals

There are times when leaving your workplace seems the only option. You've become marginalized, bored, or burned out. Perhaps your job has lost importance in the big picture. Or maybe you're simply tired of doing it. If so, consider this question: under what circumstances would you stay with the company? The answer may be: under no circumstances. But, if you can even begin to imagine a way that you could reposition yourself in the organization and consider staying, why not give it a chance? We're not talking about compromising your best work. We're talking about giving yourself a chance to create a way to do it in a familiar environment.

A recent client of ours was invited to create such an opportunity for himself after ten years with a company. Jake's performances had been poor; he was distracted and couldn't seem to keep up with the younger employees in his department. Just when he felt most discouraged and feared he would be fired, his boss surprised him. The boss explained the value the company saw in Jake's long history with the company. He admitted that the sagging performances had disappointed him in recent months, but he had a few ideas about other ways Jake could work.

Jake came to us for counsel. Could he get past the sense of failure that had been growing in him? We encouraged him to try. The company obviously valued him. A key point in Jake's "recovery" was for him to "take charge" of the creation of a new position. He wanted to regain power and prove he was worthy of the company's faith.

Jake decided to move from a financial to a sales function (one of the boss's suggestions) that would take advantage of his technical background in finding and talking to new customers. When we last met with him, he was very excited and busy making sales contacts to put his plan in action.

Not every company is so generous, but most managers know the value of retaining, reengineering, or revitalizing an employee. The cost of hiring, training, and establishing a new person is high. Keep that in mind as a real value you can offer to your employer and make the gist of your offer "I'll stay if I can offer genuine value and if we can agree on a way I can do my best work." You may be surprised by the response.

There is risk involved because you'll be making your dissatisfaction official, so be sure this is a "last ditch" moment. If the company isn't receptive, you'll know that leaving is an appropriate future direction. If you've been falling in love with more than one dream house, you'll have a few other options in the works.

▪ ORIGINAL PROJECTS ▪

Objectives

The modern workforce has become inhabited by millions of "contingency" workers. Such people work on a contracting or consulting basis according to the supply and demand of the workplace. Many people enjoy working in this autonomous manner because of the flexibility it affords and the variety of work experiences available. With the explosion of temporary employment agencies, individuals can choose to work several months at a time and, with financial planning, take time off for other things. Highly paid consultants frequently enjoy similar options—periods of intense work followed by necessary breaks to rest, recuperate, and revitalize. There are virtually no limits to the ways people can work, and the trend toward flexibility of career design is likely to increase.

If you're interested in exploring an independent work style or a part-time or part-year schedule, you may want to initiate a work proposal to a company whose needs match your skills and preferences. Another advantage of contracting work is the chance you may have to explore various companies, their cultures and values.

Once again, before initiating opportunities for contingency work, make sure you understand your objectives. Ask yourself:

· Am I hoping to expand my scope and my skills?
· Am I interested in exploring new companies or new industries?
· Do I want to keep tight control of the shape of my work? Or do I simply want to find an opportunity and see what develops?
· Is there a challenge or problem I can address for someone else while building a strong series of achievements for my résumé?
· Can I afford to work in this way?
· How can I acquire benefits such as health insurance or child care?

Our community includes several professional associations of independent consultants. Yours may, too. In your various networks you'll find other people who work on a contingency basis. Before you spend any time attempting a proposal to explore work, or before you approach an unknown but interesting client, schedule one or two informational interviews to gain insight into the process. There are also books on business development for consultants that will provide sample proposals. The most important planning for such an initiative, however, will be the groundwork you do to learn about the companies or organizations you want to approach.

Initiating an Opportunity for a Work Proposal

Who are the people you would like to work for? What industries are in need of your skills? What are their major challenges or problems, the most pressing needs of the moment? If you write a "me-centered" letter clearly stating the resources, strengths, and qualifications you offer and if the company regularly hires contractors, you may have the privilege of having your résumé filed rather than shredded. But if you write a targeted letter that shows some understanding of the company and indicates your interest in contributing to its success, you'll make a stronger connection.

You might start with a letter of approach and a request to meet with those in charge of hiring contingency employees. Find out if they have a procedure for requesting proposals or if they are open to unsolicited ones. The more information you can gain about their needs, the more specific you'll be able to be in offering your skills.

Your objective for the letter will be to introduce yourself and indicate the possibility of a match between your skills and the company's needs. Your Ah-ha résumé, formatted for this company, will be a useful document to include because proven behaviors and successful achievements establish credibility and document your talent. You may include a page of references along with summaries of recent projects if you've done some. As a relationship opens up, you'll need to follow the company's procedures for a specific work contract or seek legal advice about framing a contract of your own. Again, there are books available in the business section of libraries and bookstores with sample proposals to help you educate yourself about terms and terminology.

For now, focus on *initiating* career opportunities. If you take a few of the steps suggested, you'll easily learn about the steps that follow.

Initiating Volunteer Activity

If you want to become a volunteer for an organization that interests you or a cause you care about, you can usually take a straightforward approach. Most large agencies and institutions have formal volunteer programs, with people hired to seek willing candidates, train them, and manage their activities. Simply call to express your interest and request information about volunteer opportunities. In general, there will be forms to fill out and a meeting or gathering to provide orientation to new volunteers. You'll learn about the purpose of the organization and the tasks at hand.

If you've thought about your objectives prior to volunteering, you're likely to find more focused matches for your skills and the organization's needs. Perhaps you simply want "to be of use" and to enjoy the camaraderie of others. Volunteering can provide needed contrast to regular work, and the contrast is sometimes goal enough.

On the other hand, if you would like to build skills, face a new challenge, create a significant achievement for others, make a mark, or have an influence because you care deeply about an issue, you will want to initiate opportunity much as you would for employment. Research the organization, interview those in the know, determine the needs and challenges that your skills can address. Then meet with someone in the organization and ask if you can prepare a proposal or create a formal plan to benefit their cause. Put your skills to work in the best possible way.

Take another look at your Lifeline. The Me/Now spot is a powerful starting point. If you continue to direct your work, life, and career, you will go forward with impact. Your Lifeline will ascend whether you are being paid or not for the work you choose to do. The point is to initiate strategies for opportunity with all the power of what you know, what you value, and what you can do.

■ CONTINUING EVOLUTION OF YOUR AH-HA RÉSUMÉ ■

Objective. Tailor to specific opportunities.

Qualifications. Refine according to each exploration. Emphasize those most critical to needs of companies or organizations you're approaching.

Achievements. Select and refine for high-impact behaviors and results. Tailor selection to job functions in work-related interviews.

Employment and Related Experience. Make sure listing illustrates your best-work experience in relation to the opportunity you're exploring.

Education and Training. Continue to refine listings. Add to experience. Get advice on continuing learning in various settings.

Awards and Honors. Tailor list to interests of interviewers while retaining those that reflect your strongest qualifications. Continue "this is who I am" emphasis.

ACTION STEPS FOR INITIATING
APPROPRIATE STRATEGIES

1. Determine time and information management strategies. Select a commercial system or create one that guarantees structured time for career development.
2. Review the Interviewing for Impact Map. What contacts can you plan that will initiate action for new opportunities?

3. Begin the interviewing process, tracking and analyzing outcomes with each experience.
4. Determine additional avenues of exploration to create alternative "dream house" options. Determine two or three steps you can take to initiate activity.
5. Review your LifeCircle to explore options for volunteer proposals. Personal and community-related development will enhance your work activity and help create balance.

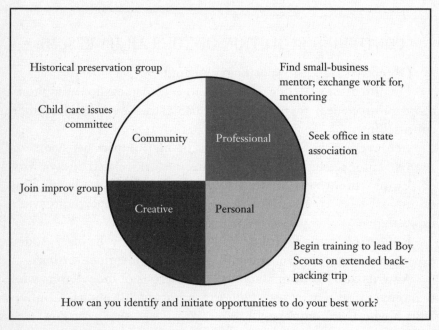

LifeCircle: Volunteer activities for best work.

ten

Professional Identity and Integrity

We often recall one of our earliest workshops. We began with a general question. Little did we know how loaded it was.

We asked the participants to briefly describe their "life and career situation" in order to set the stage for the day. We never should have included the word "life." The first person began with a health concern. Naturally, it was affecting her career, and her story began affecting all of us. She fought back tears as she described a painful, chronic illness. The next fellow was having relationship problems. Then there was the single mother with terrible financial problems. Next, a woman whose husband had recently died. It continued to go from bad to worse. When we got to the last person, we were all emotionally exhausted and needed a break. Career issues were overshadowed that day. We were too busy comforting each other and exchanging the names of doctors, counselors, and loan officers.

Although each person who attended our session that day had signed up specifically for a career strategy workshop, it was clear that other life issues, once introduced, created a greater sense of urgency. There are complex parts to people's lives that make up the whole; when one part is hurting, the other parts feel it. It's difficult to address work and career issues when other aspects of our lives need and deserve attention.

We've continued to work with a number of those participants individually as they've created or refashioned careers to fit their life circumstances. And we've changed our initial approach in a way that may be helpful to you. Now when we begin a workshop, we ask participants to take out a blank piece of paper and spend a few moments writing down all the life issues that they feel need to be addressed. Then we say, ever so gently, "Now take the paper, fold it up, and slip it into the pocket of your notebook. Those are important issues, but they are not the ones we're addressing today. Today we will focus on career issues, with the understanding that you'll be working on the other aspects of your life as you develop new directions for your work."

We offer to make referrals in private for those needing expert assistance with financial, emotional, relationship, health, and other issues, but we don't integrate them directly during our time together. We want those who are striving to do the best work of their lives to operate from an assumption of power, competence, and authority in relation to their careers. The vulnerabilities are still there, but we've literally put them out of sight. Over time we've learned that our wise participants can manage to integrate their other issues on their own, privately. We don't need to remind them.

If integration means the combination of parts into a complete and harmonious whole, a unification through mutual adjustment, then most of us aren't fully integrated most of the time. Our LifeCircles, as we've examined them in this book, remind us of how little time we may spend on creative endeavors or community involvement. There's always more we can do to develop our personal lives. If we exercise enough, we don't spend enough time with the kids. Too much time with the kids and we begin to yearn for time with a book, a grown-up book. To focus on work, then, seems one more way of compartmentalizing our lives.

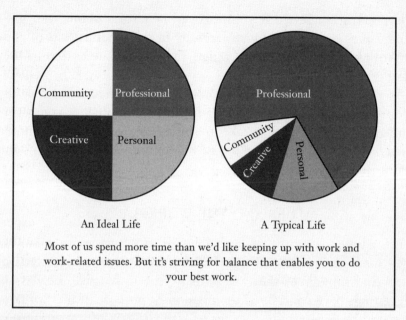

An Ideal Life · A Typical Life

Most of us spend more time than we'd like keeping up with work and work-related issues. But it's striving for balance that enables you to do your best work.

LifeCircle: Balanced and unbalanced.

▪ VALUES AND IDENTITY ▪

Perhaps we'll never strike a perfect balance in time and activity. There's opportunity for an integration, however, in recognizing our governing values and cultivating a habit of integrity. The habit comes from awareness and purpose. Why am I doing this? Why am I doing that? What should I do next? What will inform my decision?

Throughout the earlier chapters of this book, we've worked to establish an ongoing habit of gaining clarity about ourselves and our goals and creating a strategy to direct our lives, through our work, toward an integrated vision. We've become very specific in the tools and tactics needed to move ahead with our plan.

It's time to ask again, "What values will inform my decision?" The piece of paper with your other life issues carefully listed is important. You will not be able to go forward freely in your work without continuously gaining clarity and creating strategies to address other issues as well. Your new habits will serve your life well. As you proceed diligently to understand yourself and your vision for work, don't be surprised if you begin to be clearer about your governing values and to plan more carefully in the other aspects of your life. Work has the power to embolden, to bring resources to the other challenges we face.

As you explore ways to work in the future, understand that the professional identity you develop can add to and influence your overall integrity. The actions you take to explore future work, then, should be tied not simply to ambition but to an identity you want to grow and nurture.

▪ VALUES AND THE WORKPLACE ▪

From time to time we've mentioned values in relation to the workplace. Some companies or organizations have formal statements of values. And sometimes they are actually true in practice. Leaders in such settings have considered the mission or purpose of their organization and have determined values or standards to inform employees and others of the expectations held by management, boards of direc-

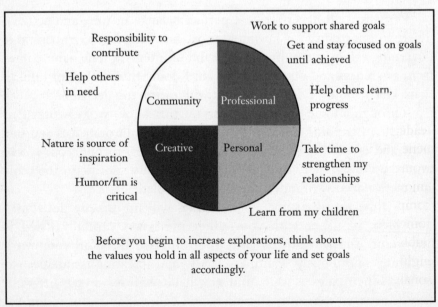

LifeCircle: Governing values.

tors, and other governing bodies. Sometimes the values reflect directly the work that has to be done. A manufacturing firm might state such values as "health- and safety-conscious, loyal, and productive." Many companies today state outright that they require "flexibility and collaboration" as work-related values. Some, such as academic departments, museums, and other cultural organizations expect civility without necessarily saying so. A boisterous, fun-loving person who enjoys practical jokes as part of his or her work experience would generally do well to look elsewhere for employment. Finding an organization that matches your values is an important part of working with integrity.

> **So We Asked an Expert.** Ellen E. Wood, Human Resources Coordinator, Grant Thornton, LLP, International, says: "Sometimes applicants say 'Tell me about the culture of your organization.' I'm impressed by that."
>
> **The Point:** Executives want people who will fit into their established culture. By showing interest, you demonstrate insight about the importance of the work environment.

We regularly appear on a local television affiliate as workplace experts. Our challenge for each segment is to find an important work issue and, true to television format, address it in an entertaining way in seven minutes. Recently, we chose to address the issue of values. We asked viewers this question: "If your workplace had a personality, what would it be?" (Secretly, we wanted to add, "And would it be a personality you'd want to hang out with?")

We tried the question out on a number of friends before the show. One of them, a corporate project leader, said his company would be a stuffy guy in a navy-blue suit, benevolent but distant. Another, more alarming response came from a woman who works for a very entrepreneurial company that has enjoyed rapid growth through, we learned, ruthless opportunism. "My company would be a guy in a bar, wearing gold chains, trying to pick someone up." Other descriptions included "giddy and shallow" (a public relations concern) and "deep and troubled" (a dysfunctional but highly regarded medical practice). Other people described the personality of their workplaces as congenial, nurturing, bright, or optimistic.

As you continue to clarify past experiences to help focus future goals, consider the values question. How would you describe workplace values you've experienced? What were the "personalities" of the organizations in which you did your best work? What are your values in relation to the way you like to work?

The question begins to broaden as you remember and consider work environments. The atmosphere and style of a workplace is often a signal of underlying values, just as your personality and style represent, consciously or not, your values.

Quite frequently, female clients seeking to leave corporate or highly professional positions admit that they are looking for a workplace that won't require wearing panty hose. We used to laugh, but we have learned that this is a serious statement. The formal, confining, armored-body feeling they are interested in discarding often reflects the structure of jobs that have lost their luster. Mercifully, many of the most sophisticated work environments today have become at least somewhat more casual, a trend attributed to the number of baby boomers at the helm.

Your task is to use your recent review of past work history, your exploration of skills, and your recognition of preferences to gain understanding about your values and style and their relation to future work environments. When we're asked by job seekers whether they should wear a suit to an interview, we always say yes. And we advise women to wear skirted suits, not pants. But we're reluctant to get much more specific than that. Instead, we suggest the conventional outfit as a way to reduce distraction and to offend no one. But we counsel clients to pay attention to the environment when they arrive for their interview and try to determine the prevailing styles of dress and behavior. Then we urge them to assess whether

So We Asked an Expert. Diane J. Frisch, Vice-President of Human Resources, Alumax Mill Products, Inc., states: "Professionalism in a prospective employee is the whole package—presence, what they've been doing with their life, professional growth outside the job."

The Point: The best companies are looking for people with a wide array of interests and activities. What you do off the job says a lot about what you'll do on the job.

or not they would fit in. Often it's possible to initiate a discussion about values and workplace style in an interview. The more you can find out, the better able you'll be to determine if you've found a match.

If you're feeling "unprofessional" in your personal image or are entering a new field and are uncertain about standards of appearance, pay attention to that. Your professional identity will be influenced by how you look. Grooming, clothing choices, and appropriate accessories are addressed in many current business-image books. We aren't fashion experts. But, in keeping with our philosophy about work, we encourage you to determine the difference between fashion and style and to cultivate a style that reflects who you are and respects the environment you ultimately choose for your work.

▪ IDENTITY AND INTEGRITY: THE LONG VIEW ▪

In Chapter 2 we suggested a process of steps you could take between the Me/Now spot on your Lifeline and the possible visions you could create for your future. We asked you to get scared about the urgency of time. We wanted you to pencil in some possibilities for the future, just to begin giving shape to your goals. We reminded you to be serious but not too serious. To pay attention to the changing nature of the workplace in order to understand that, if there's a constant, it's *you*.

So We Asked an Expert. Jodie Grubbs, Human Resources, Target Stores, says: "In an interview, to assess professionalism in a prospective employee, we look for competence in a lot of different experiences. Whether they are a solid communicator and express ideas clearly. Integrity and dependability are important."

The Point: It's quite clear.

The ultimate point was then, as now, that your current reality, the Me/Now spot on your Lifeline, is the stepping-off place toward a new vision. The Me/Now on your Lifeline should be far better defined in your thinking at this point. The vision of how you'd like to work should be coming into focus, along with your strategies, and the informed actions you'll be taking will give you even more focus.

The values you hold will be a

strong checkpoint as your options unfold. You'll find that, after every two or three steps you take, you'll need to reclarify direction.

Why am I doing this? What will be the purpose if I offer my best work here? You'll be likely to answer those questions easily, but it's vital that you remember to ask them. The best work of your life will be both excellent and personally satisfying. Get totally involved in it as long as it moves toward your vision.

However, if you get sidetracked, get back on your Lifeline and take control. If your work becomes less than your best, get out your LifeCircle and find another part of your life in which to put your values to work. Look for the people who like themselves, who work with satisfaction. Collect the stories that inspire you and remind you of the value of your time.

Professional Identity and Integrity: Examples That Inspire Us

There is no one in the following series of descriptions who wouldn't be immediately known as someone of integrity and strong professional identity. We suspect that the sense of identity in each case did not begin in the workplace. Some of the best work that inspires people occurs outside of employment settings, with or without public recognition. Sometimes it even continues as others carry out their vision. The integration of governing values in each of our examples has made these individuals notable and created inspiration for others.

Nancy Denney died nearly three years ago, but her best work continues. A professor at a major university, Nancy struggled as a single parent to gain tenure and over time became a leader in changing policy affecting women's pay equity on her campus. She was controversial, brave, outspoken, and joyous. As she fought and ultimately lost a battle with cancer, she continued to work toward her dream: to establish a house for undergraduate students who are single parents, to offer them a home and the cooperative support that she had lacked in her own experience. Less than two years after her death, we attended the ribbon-cutting ceremony of the Nancy Denney House. A complex vision layered with business planning, major fund-raising, research and policy-making, communication systems, and finally scrubbing, painting, and furnishing a home was completed by a handful of the busiest women in town. Nancy's friends, already overburdened in their lives and careers, were infused with her values, her example, and, some believe, an impatient power pushing them from beyond to get the work done.

Ron, an editor at a publishing house, is well established and respected in his career. His work long ago ceased to be the only occupation he has. His devotion to others is legendary. Several years ago a friend, a woman of forty, mentioned that she hoped someday to find her birth mother. Ron initiated an arduous strategy, devoting one evening a week to the necessary research of files in the New York Public Library. After several months, he found the matching birth records and created the contacts necessary for a deeply appreciated reunion. He has since found two other lost family members for friends.

Phil and Renee took a long look at the right side of their Lifelines and realized that they were in a peculiar stage. Energetic, retired early, they had grown, unmarried children and no grandchildren on the horizon. They saw the proverbial window of opportunity. They signed up for the Peace Corps—surprising the kids, the neighbors, and even themselves, according to Renee. They have recently returned from two years in rural Poland and have decided to pursue at least one more tour of duty before settling back in.

Rachel, new to the workforce and on her own for the first time, realized that her life could quickly fill up with the friends she was meeting and the interesting cultural events in her new city. Before her social life took over (as it had many times before), she signed up with an AIDS support network and soon became the Saturday companion of Stephen, who was slowly dying. She knew him for a year and considered it a privilege to be a part of his last months. She addressed a deep need to get beyond the ordinary in some part of her life. In Stephen she found a friend and a mirror in which to see a new side of herself.

Susie decided several years ago to learn about gardening systematically. She's a full-time nurse, but the passion for her new best work took her by storm. She found abundant opportunities to join associations and clubs to meet horticulturists, study everything she could about indigenous plants and flowers, and explore the international subculture of other passionate gardeners. In time she decided to develop a business so she could teach others about the things she'd learned. She calls the business Garden Partners. She accepts a few clients each season who can fit around her busy work schedule, and together (as partners) they study the yard and explore options for new designs. Together they work the soil, together they learn, and together they enjoy the triumph of a growing season. Susie grows relationships and offers nurturing collaborations as a nurse and as a gardening consultant.

Fran retired to Washington, D.C., from California at the age of seventy. She spent the next fifteen years fulfilling a dream. She had always wanted to experience life in the heart of a political culture. She moved to the hub of the city, got into the middle of campaigns that interested her, and experienced a vision she had long held. Just when most people feel marginalized, Fran got to the center of things, got involved, and got to know a whole new world of people and projects. She had a lifetime of skills to offer. At eighty-five she moved back to California to retire again and be near her family.

> **So We Asked an Expert:** Rebecca Chekouras, Director of Development, San Francisco Women's Philharmonic., states: "Change happens gracefully when the spirit you have been tending internally demands expression in the outside world. All of your previous work experience has been an incubation of this new self and can now be put to service in its birth. Your history is your apprenticeship to your future."
>
> **The Point:** You've been preparing for your best work for a long time.

Maureen tried a number of careers before settling, once and for all, on that of beautician. She had found that transforming the way people looked felt like magic to her and made them feel wonderful, too. She cherishes the relationships she's built over the years with her customers. Mostly, though, Maureen is a woman with a lively intellect. Few of her customers know the extent of her self-made curriculum. Maureen subscribes to two daily newspapers, which she reads religiously. She has become a sculptor. She's studied about opera and attends performances regularly. She loves her work because it frees her mind for the passions she pursues when the workday is done. Her best work supports her love for learning.

Lifeline/Integrity, LifeCircle/Identity

The tools we've used in this book are simple constructs: a line, a circle. If they've become a part of your thinking, as they have ours, remember to use them as you move forward to find your best work.

Your Lifeline will help remind you about integrity. Complete and undivided wholeness. The integration of all you can know in knowing yourself. The LifeCircle will remind you of the many sources of your identity. The standards you set as your work goes along and the presence you establish will mark you as a talent, a person who is useful, and you'll be drawn willingly into service in surprising ways. Your best work will always be whatever work serves the purposes of your life and uses your best strengths.

ACTION STEPS FOR ESTABLISHING PROFESSIONAL IDENTITY AND INTEGRITY

1. On a blank piece of paper, make a list of all the issues you need to address. Think about health, finance, relationships, and other issues that arise and distract you, however rightfully, from career issues. Fold the paper carefully and put it in a place you will remember. As you address career planning strategies, leave the list of issues safely tucked away. Address the issues at another time, using the Clarity, Strategy, and Action approach.
2. Describe the "personality" of the places you've worked in the past. Make notes about the compatibility or discomfort you felt in those environments. What are the values you seek in a work environment? How will you know them when you see them?
3. Create a fresh copy of your Lifeline and LifeCircle. Make notes that will help you remember to integrate your values in work considerations. Make additional notes about your sense of identity. How do you want to present yourself in new work settings?

4. Make a list of people you know who seem to be happy, who enjoy themselves, and whom you admire. Include meetings with these people when possible as you move forward in your search for important career information. Inspiration is important.

Part III

ACTION

So far we've discussed Clarity and Strategy. Now it's time for Action. By this point you should be fairly clear about what you have to offer in the workplace, based on what you've learned in the first part of the book. You should have identified your strengths, skills, and abilities, uncovered your values, and decided on the way you prefer to work. In the second part of the book you should have developed your Ah-ha résumé. You should be fairly secure in knowing that you want to make a change, and you even may have mapped out a strategy for beginning the process of change. The next step, covered in this section, is preparing to take action.

If you jumped straight to "Action" without first gaining clarity and deciding on a strategy, then you may be searching for the easy way into a new job. Guess what? There is no easy way. We strongly urge you to go back and read through the first two parts of the book so that you'll be ready to take deliberate and appropriate action. The time you spend gaining clarity and developing a strategy now will save you from being sidetracked by an unsatisfying job, only to be on the market again in a few years.

A word about time here. When we first started working on this book, we were amazed at all of the resources available to someone searching for employment. Early in the development of the book, we decided to search the Internet for career-related information. Five hours later we looked up and emerged from virtual career land with more confusion than anything else. We'd barely touched on all the sites that came up from a search of the word "career," and we hadn't even gotten to searching "job" yet. The same thing happened at the library when we became enmeshed in stacks and stacks of books and reference materials on the subject of careers.

Some people like doing research and enjoy the technical details of finding information, so they don't mind getting lost in the morass and spending hours on-line or in the library. However, if your time is limited or if you don't particularly care for that kind of activity, then make sure you watch the clock very carefully. Set a limit for how long you'll stay at the library. Put a timer next to your computer and get off the Web when it rings. If you go overboard one day, you may convince yourself that you don't have the time to develop a careful career or job change process. You do have the time, just regulate it.

We think we've come up with a way to present information on necessary action steps without overwhelming you. We decided not to compile exhaustive lists of resources, because new ones come and old ones go all the time. Instead, we'll show you the *process* of using resources to take action toward finding your best work. We hope that you'll adapt the process to suit your needs. We'll also try to give you an indication of the time involved in taking different kinds of action. And we'll introduce you to four individuals who differ in life stage, socioeconomic level, and skill background.

As we move through the remaining chapters, the activities of these four individuals will provide examples of specific uses of the types of resources discussed. We invite you to get involved with the stories of these people, experience the process of career exploration with them, and consider what you will do with your exploration as you read through these chapters and map out a strategy for action.

▪ CAST OF CHARACTERS ▪

Ana

Ana is a beginner. She is twenty-three, just out of college, and ready to search for her first "real" job. She has been living at home working at a retail store for a year and is now moving to Cleveland with her boyfriend, who is starting graduate school. During this past year Ana was able to save enough money to buy her first car, used but serviceable. Ana had also decided she wanted to save enough money so that she could afford to move and spend some time looking for a career position. By the end of the year she figured she had been able to put away money to live on for about two months, though she hoped it would not take her that long to find a job. Monthly payments for the carryover health benefits from her retail position would quickly eat away her savings. She's flexible about the type of position she'd like, although she's discovered that she doesn't like retail or sales. She was a liberal arts major in college and she wants to use her leadership and organizational skills to start building a career.

Sam

Sam is a striver. He is thirty-five, a high school graduate with an Automobile Service Excellence (ASE) certificate who's been working as an auto mechanic at the local service station for ten years. He's married to Tonya, who does child care in their home, and they have a two-year-old son. Sam has always loved working on cars and he's very proud of his mechanical abilities. He takes pleasure in getting to know the customers and being able to help them solve their automotive problems. He dreams about being his own boss and has decided that the time is right to make a change, before his family and his responsibilities grow.

Paula

Paula is a professional. At forty-two she "has it all"—a master's degree in business administration, a fifteen-year career in financial services, a husband who's a district attorney, and two teenage children. She's been moving ahead in her career consistently through the years and has been fortunate to have had quality child care and an understanding spouse who is just as busy building his own career. She usually works twelve-hour days and at least part of every weekend. A tribute to her commitment, her company has just offered her a prestigious promotion with a sizable salary increase—at the home office a hundred miles away.

She loves her career, her job, and her company, and she has always positioned herself for advancement, but she won't uproot her family. In fact, this opportunity has made her question the way she has been working, and she longs for some balance between career and family. She's missing much of her children's last years at home. In addition, Paula's parents aren't getting any younger, and her father's heart condition has made him quite vulnerable.

Lamarr

Lamarr is raring for retirement. He's fifty-five, and he and his wife, Andrea, have three grown children. Lamarr has worked for the city government for thirty-three years and is planning to take early retirement. The lack of appreciation for his intellect has made him extremely cynical about his workplace, and a recent heart attack indicated that the stress of his job was taking its toll. He has now regained his health and is looking forward to retirement to do what he really wants. Unfortunately, even though he has a reasonable pension, Lamarr and Andrea can't get by on her part-time salary as a kindergarten teacher at the local elementary school.

Lamarr's passion has been model trains, and he has amassed a large collection of antique train sets, many of which are very valuable. He tends to be a solitary fellow who loves to read train magazines, and he is wondering whether he can turn his avocation into a retirement career.

▪ WHAT ABOUT YOU? ▪

Summarize your situation in a paragraph or two. Are you a beginner, looking for a first job, changing jobs, or reentering the job market? Are you a striver, wanting to get ahead in the working world, perhaps moving from being an employee to being an employer? Are you a professional trying to put balance into your life while positioning yourself for career advancement? Or are you thinking about a retirement career, a career change, or reinventing the way you work? From the examples that will follow of how Ana, Sam, Paula, and Lamarr use job search resources, we hope you can determine better the action you will take to carry out your career strategies.

eleven

Printed Material

The time you spend perusing printed material can vary from skimming an annual report to reading everything you can about an industry or occupation. Decide in advance how much time you want to spend in the bookstore or at the library on each visit, then stick to your limit. And always ask for help from a reference librarian or a bookstore salesperson, so you can use your time more effectively and efficiently.

Printed material to help you in your job search is abundant. The first part of this chapter will provide you with an overview of sources for printed material and how to locate and use them. The second part will give you examples of how Ana, Sam, Paula, and Lamarr used printed material in their job searches, so you can form ideas about locating and using information for your own specific needs.

▪ SOURCES FOR PRINTED MATERIAL ▪

Library

A library is the most complete source of printed reference material. To begin your research on careers and jobs, you must first select an appropriate library. Generally speaking, there are four types of library systems: public libraries, college and university libraries, corporate libraries (for example, the local newspaper), and government libraries (for example, the state historical society or state law library). If your local public library is too limited for your purposes, you may have to travel to a large urban public library or to a college library. If travel would be difficult, your local reference librarian may be able to place a special request with a larger library system for certain items you want to see. If a college or university limits access to its library, you can usually obtain a one-day pass. (Don't hesitate to ask: if it's a public institution, it's using some of your tax dollars.) That pass should allow you access to the collections, but will not include borrowing privileges. (That's okay, because reference material can't be checked out anyway. Always bring enough change for the photocopy machine.) Corporate and government librarians can usually arrange for use of their libraries if you call in advance.

As soon as you arrive at the library, locate the reference librarian, state that you are beginning a job search, and ask for an overview of the pertinent reference materials. The job of the reference librarian is to help you in your search for information. If you go to the library in person, the reference librarian will point you in the right direction and let you sort through and interpret the information yourself. If you contact the reference librarian by telephone with a specific question, you will get the information you request and usually some type of interpretation.

To make the best use of the reference materials, your library research should begin with getting a broad picture of an industry or occupation. Then proceed to making comparisons among industry competitors or occupational settings. Conclude with focusing on an individual company or employer. The reference librarian can introduce you to the reference tools you will need to do this, so don't hesitate to ask for help.

If you're considering specific businesses or organizations, write or telephone them directly for more detailed information than you're likely to find in the library—brochures, annual reports, background information, etc. You can get the addresses from the reference librarian.

One of our clients who lives in a small town decided to check out the local library to see what references were available. Unfortunately, the library had restricted hours, and this individual learned that the resources of this library were, as they said, "limited." Our client found out that most area residents who need to research printed material make a twenty-five-mile trip to a town with a medium-sized library or even the forty-mile trip to a larger town with a more extensive collection in their municipal library. Those who are reluctant or unable to drive to a larger town are often able to use the library at the area middle school or high school. High schools, particularly, will have some good reference materials, and you can sometimes gain access by calling the school librarian and requesting a visit at the end of the school day.

Bookstore

In addition to the library, printed materials are available from other sources. Bookstores carry a selection of career-related books, job search guides, and reference materials. Caution: select wisely—you could spend all of your time reading about careers instead of developing one.

Business periodicals, professional association publications, and trade journals may be available in some bookstores and libraries. If not, you can usually buy them directly from the publisher. Most, if not all, issues contain a listing of job openings; many have special issues that cover salaries and job trends in the field. You can get information about ordering single issues by calling the national association representing specialists in your area of interest (e.g., American Management Association, National Association of Health Care Professionals, American Society of Travel Agents). National associations also have membership directories that may be available for purchase. These directories can provide you with names and addresses of contacts working in the field. Usually there are listings by geography and sub-specialty.

Newsstand

You can pick up newspapers and weekly business magazines at your local newsstand or bookstore, if your libraries don't subscribe to them or if it's more convenient. Reading the business section of a national newspaper can provide you with insight into overall industry and job trends, as can the weekly business magazines. The *National Business Employment Weekly* provides invaluable career tips and a view of the current business scene.

▪ HOW JOB SEEKERS USE PRINTED MATERIALS ▪

To show how you can use the information you've acquired, let's look at how our four job seekers have been using printed materials in their job search efforts.

Ana began her job search by going to the local bookstore and spending an hour looking through the titles in the career section. She found a book called the *Cleveland Job Bank*. It didn't have current job listings, of course, but she skimmed it and thought it would give her a sense of what types of employers were in the area, so she bought it. She also bought a map of Cleveland so she could get oriented to her new location. (If you belong to an automobile club, take advantage of their services to gather as much information as you can about prospective locations.) In addition, she called the reference librarian at the local library for the address of the Cleveland Chamber of Commerce and wrote for general information on the city. When she and her boyfriend made a preliminary trip to Cleveland to find an apartment, she bought a copy of the Sunday *Cleveland Plain Dealer* so she could check out the classifieds and see what types of jobs were advertised.

Sam was certified in auto mechanics by the National Institute for Automotive Service Excellence (ASE) and received its semiannual publication, the *Blue Seal*. He began setting aside time in the evenings to look over the section on employment opportunities in back issues. Nothing had strong appeal because he really harbored a dream of owning his own service station. He went to the library one Saturday morning and asked the reference librarian to help him find out whether there was a trade association for service station owners, and she directed him to a number of reference books.

The *National Trade and Professional Associations of the United States* (Columbia Books, Inc.), an annual publication, was the first book he chose. This is a comprehensive reference of trade and professional associations with six useful indices, so Sam was able to look up references by association name, subject, geographical location, budget level, name of the association executive, or association acronym (such as ASE). Because he didn't know if there was a trade association for service station owners, he began by looking in the subject index under "gasoline." He found listings for the American Truck Stop Operators Association, the Society of Independent Gasoline Marketers of America, and two others that looked particularly interesting: the Gasoline and Automotive Service Dealers Association and the Service Station Dealers of America and Allied Trades (SSDA), which offer information, professional development, and new opportunities to service station dealers.

Sam copied the address, telephone number, and name of the association executive for each of these entries. His plan was to write for information and request recent publications so that he could get a feel for the issues facing service station owners.

He next checked under the subject heading "automobiles" and found a related entry—the Automotive Service Association (ASA), which represents businesses providing automobile service. Even though he was more interested in a full-service gas station than an automotive repair business, Sam took down the contact information, including an electronic-mail address and a World Wide Web address.

To make sure he hadn't missed anything, he also looked under "garages" and added information to his list about the Convenient Automotive Services Institute, on the outside chance that he might develop an interest in owning a gas station/convenience store combination. He checked the *Encyclopedia of Associations* (Gale Research Publications) and found that he had covered all relevant organizations. He was amazed by all that he'd learned so far.

The reference librarian had also given Sam the *Small Business Sourcebook, volumes 1 and 2* (Gale Research Publications). Because he didn't have a specific small business to research in the master list of small-business profiles, he searched under the general heading "Service Station/Auto Repair and Service Shop" and found a wealth of information organized under twelve main sections:

· Start-up information
· Directories of educational programs

· Reference works
· Sources of supply
· Statistical sources
· Trade periodicals
· Videocassettes/audiocassettes
· Trade shows and conventions
· Consultants
· Franchises and business opportunities
· Computerized databases
· Computer systems/software

Sam photocopied the pages from this section so that he could thoroughly review the information at home. He also checked out *Mancuso's Small Business Resource Guide* (Small Business Sourcebooks) and *The Insider's Guide to Small Business Resources* (Doubleday). After spending about two hours in the library, he went home with a great deal of information to consider and a better feeling about his career ideas.

Paula had already decided she would turn down the promotion offered by her company, because she didn't want to move her family or commute. She had a dilemma. She wanted to cut back her work to a reasonable forty hours per week while at the same time positioning herself for continued advancement in her company. She felt strongly about both goals and hoped others would recognize her value to the company and would respect her priorities. She thought that a way to reach her goals might be to narrow her professional focus and become more of a specialist in one area.

To develop a compelling proposal, she needed to know more about the current issues affecting the financial industry and select one to pursue. She paid close attention to discussions of job trends in the *Wall Street Journal* and business publications like *BusinessWeek* and *Fortune*. She went to the library of the local business school and spent an hour looking at recent business journals to identify the hot topics affecting the financial industry. She also went to her local public library and checked out *The Directory of Executive Recruiters* (Kennedy

Publications) and *The Guide to Executive Recruiters* (McGraw-Hill). She decided that she should test her market value and see whether there were other firms that would be interested in someone with her skills. These books also provided basic information on the different types of search firms (headhunters) and tips on how to interact with them. She never seemed to have a block of time to devote to uninterrupted reading. She simply had to grab an hour here or there whenever she could.

Lamarr wanted to correspond with people who shared an interest in model trains, but he didn't know how to find them. He subscribed to *Model Railroader Magazine*, but he had become increasingly restless and was ready to start interacting with other collectors rather than just reading about them. When he went to his local public library, the reference librarian suggested that he look in the *Encyclopedia of Associations* (Gale Research Publications), because it includes educational, hobby, and avocational organizations, both national and international. He found a reference for the National Model Railroad Association (NMRA), which has thousands of members and publishes the *NMRA Bulletin* monthly, as well as a number of smaller regional and special interest group newsletters. He copied all the information for this entry and wrote for a membership application. Through this organization he'd be able to keep abreast of conferences, workshops, and seminars and develop a network of contacts. This trip to the library took him less than thirty minutes.

From these examples, you should be starting to get some ideas of how you can use printed material to get job and career information. You may find yourself returning again and again to the library as you uncover information that you want to clarify or expand upon. For example, suppose that you've decided you want to move to San Francisco and work in retail. You can look in the *Directory of Advertisers* to locate all of the retail stores in the Bay Area. You'll narrow your focus and have a valuable foundation for beginning informational interviews. If you're in Chicago and you want to make a career change from finance into insurance, you can look in the *Directory of Insurance Companies* to make a list of businesses you're interested in investigating

further. If in the next chapter (electronic information) you find reference to certain organizations you want to know more about, you can
call the reference librarian and request a photocopy of the relevant
material. The skills and resources of a reference librarian will amaze
you.

twelve

Electronic Information

If you've never accessed the Internet, beware! It takes time. We don't mean time to learn how to get onto the World Wide Web (Web) and navigate around all of the sites out there. That's fairly straightforward. But because there's so much information, it's very easy to get lost in time, so be careful.

In case the Internet and the Web are foreign to you, here are the basics: to connect to the Internet, you need a computer with a modem and software that will allow you to connect by phone line to a central server or service provider. This software will have some type of browser (like Netscape Navigator or Microsoft Explorer) that will enable you to explore the World Wide Web, a part of the Internet in which text, expressive lettering, art, photos, color, sound, animation, and forms are linked. The result: you can explore sites interactively, choosing whatever information you want and going wherever your interests and curiosity take you.

Think of the World Wide Web as a spiderweb, with spokes that radiate out from a center and are joined by concentric circles. All of the information is arranged so that you can gain access to it in levels, both directly and indirectly. Web pages are written in hypertext, a language that allows links between keywords and phrases, between related concepts and issues, so a user can jump from site to site pursuing information on a particular topic or keyword.

If you are interested in going directly to specific information, you can use one of the many search engines on the Web, such as Yahoo!, Lycos, and Infoseek. They are easily accessible from the home page that first appears when you access the Web. Using a search engine gives you a choice of hunting techniques: choosing a topic from a directory (a listing of categories by subject or region) or choosing a topic by query (a search by the keyword or keywords you type in).

Search engines vary in ease of use. They vary also in the amount of information they offer the user. So prepare to be overwhelmed; then learn how to use the engines for more sophisticated, efficient searches. The results will be well worth the time you spend.

There are a number of ways you can access on-line career and job information. If you already have a computer, a modem, and Internet access, then you're set to use the information listed in this chapter. On the other hand, if you think a modem is a modern form of totem and on-line means standing in a store and waiting for service, then you have only two choices: ask your six-year-old neighbor or grandchild to help you access the Web on his or her computer, or ask a reference librarian to show you how to use the library's on-line services. If you're eager to go solo, seek out a knowledgeable Internet user to show you the ropes, or attend classes on using the Internet, offered at adult and continuing education programs in most communities.

If you have a computer and a modem but no access, then you need an account with an Internet service provider. You can subscribe to a major provider, such as America Online, Compuserve, or Prodigy, or look up Internet service providers in the yellow pages of your local telephone directory. A phone call will give you the information you need to get connected. Most providers offer similar services, but some are more customer-friendly than others and the charges may vary widely.

If you don't have a computer or a modem or you can't afford the access charges, don't worry. You don't need to miss out on all the benefits of cyberspace. Your local library may have computers for patrons to use to access the Internet. If not, there may be a computer that will allow you at least to do an on-line search of resources at that particular library or library system. The reference librarian can guide you through either process. If you're in a very small town and your public library does not have access to the Internet, you may be able to use the computers at your local public school. Call the school librarian and ask whether he or she has time to show you how to search the Web some-day after school hours.

▪ CYBERSPACE: A WORLD OF INFORMATION AND OPPORTUNITIES ▪

Once you gain access to the Internet, you'll find an overwhelming number of sites on the World Wide Web that are related to careers and jobs. Before you get started you may want to browse the printed Internet directories available at the library or local bookstore. For example, *The Internet Yellow Pages* (Osborne, McGraw-Hill) has a "jobs" heading, with a number of subheadings that lead you to Web sites in categories such as "academic jobs," "contract labor," "employer profiles," and "professional career organizations." There are even books that will give you specific information on how to use the Internet for your job search, such as *Finding a Job on the Internet* (Glossbrenner & Glossbrenner) and *The Guide to Internet Job Search-ing* (Roehm, Oserman, & Riley).

One point to keep in mind: things change fast on the Internet. Even the latest book won't be up to date. Web sites are being devel-oped and expanded at an amazing rate, they move frequently to another address, and some change names. But once you're familiar with navigating the Web, you'll find out about sites not listed in the books and you'll learn ways to find even more sites.

In the following pages we're going to cover various types of sites to give you an idea of what you can find on the Web. Then we'll show how our four characters use the Internet to develop their careers and find their best work.

Experienced Web surfers will have noticed by now that we do not include the URL, or Universal Resource Locator, for most of the Web sites we mention. We decided that it is much easier to learn about the *process* of searching the Web than it is to type in, error-free, addresses such as *http://www.yahoo.com/Education/Guidance/Career_and_Employ-*

ment_Planning/. Besides, as we mentioned above, Web sites often change addresses and new sites are added continually, so you will be more efficient knowing the search process than being provided with Web addresses.

Resource Lists

Starting with Web addresses from printed sources, such as the books cited above, you can use on-line resource lists to create a short list of sites that seem most relevant to your specific needs and interests. A resource list is a Web site that directs you to other sources of information, using links.

You'll find some sites that are focused on career information and some that contain job listings. Scroll through the list of resource links and click on underlined or highlighted items (the links) to transfer directly to that destination. If the site looks good and you want to come back to it later, you can make the return visit easier by setting a bookmark (using a tool that is part of your browser, you can store links to your favorite sites and go to them directly from your bookmark file). Using a resource list is an efficient way to begin narrowing your search.

Career Centers

The next level of useful sites consists of the on-line career centers. These sites provide a wealth of information on occupations, employers, and jobs. Many also offer traditional career counseling tips on résumé writing, interviewing techniques, and general job search skills. The federal government maintains a Federal Job Opportunities Electronic Bulletin Board at (912) 757–3100 as well as an Internet site at *http://www.usajobs.opm.gov.*

Job Banks

Job banks are Web sites that are like the classified ads in the newspaper. They offer job listings in an organized fashion, usually by geographical location, type of work, keyword, and company name. Some job banks are merely listings of information, but some of the sites will let you enter your qualifications and preferences and will match you with specific employers.

If you're interested in local opportunities, you may be able to find a job bank set up to serve your metropolitan area, county, or section of the state. If your city or county has a home page, that's a good place to start looking. (A home page is like the front of a brochure, with links to the pages inside the brochure.) Many cities now have home pages on the World Wide Web, where you can find out almost anything, from the name of the mayor to the best place to buy fishing bait, and many include a local job bank.

Résumé Banks

Résumé banks are screening tools for employers. You either upload a file of your résumé onto the site or fill out an on-line form that creates a standardized résumé. ("Upload" means to bring up a file on your smaller computer and load or transfer it onto another, larger computer, such as your Internet server. This is relatively easy with browsers such as Netscape Navigator or Microsoft Explorer. You may first need to save your file in ASCII format, rather than as you'd usually save it with your word processor, but that's a simple matter.)

An employer who accesses the résumé banks uses keywords to describe a position opening, then the computer scans through the résumé database to find keyword matches. In order for your résumé to be selected, it's important to include specific words and phrases that describe your skills and job preferences, such as systems analyst, LPN experienced in home health care, pharmaceutical sales, and so on. If there is a match, the employer can download a copy of your résumé and contact you directly. ("Download" means to load a file from the Internet server, a larger computer, and bring it down to your smaller computer.) If you're currently employed and checking out your options elsewhere, you should use caution. Most résumé banks have a system to preserve confidentiality, but it's conceivable that your present employer could request a keyword search, find your résumé, and identify you by your experience.

USENET Newsgroups and Discussion Lists

USENET newsgroups offer on-line advice and support on many job and career issues. You can join a discussion group on a certain topic, post questions or answers on a bulletin board, or just check for information from other job seekers. You can access USENET newsgroups through the World Wide Web or through a news server. (Check with your on-line service provider for information specific to your system.) One popular group is *misc.jobs.misc*, touted as the place to talk and trade tips about employment, the workplace, and careers.

Similar to newsgroups are discussion lists, also known as LIST-SERVs, which operate through electronic mail. There are thousands of discussion lists and several good search engines on the Web to help you locate the ones you need. For example, *http://tile.net* is the Comprehensive Internet Reference to Discussion Lists. This site also allows searching for USENET newsgroups.

If you want to participate in a discussion group, you send an e-mail message to the indicated server address with the wording they specify. After you subscribe, you get e-mail every time a list member wants to share information or opinions. If you want to join the discussion, you can send a message either to the whole group or just to certain members. (How you do this depends on your e-mail program.)

USENET newsgroups and discussion lists allow you to join networks that can stretch around the world, but you can also find some that are more local in scope. They're basically cyber communities of people sharing what they know and helping each other.

▪ HOW JOB SEEKERS USE ELECTRONIC INFORMATION ▪

Once you get access to the Internet, how you use it depends on your needs and interests, and how active and creative you can be. Here are examples from Ana, Sam, Paula, and Lamarr.

Ana was very familiar with the Internet because she'd spent time in college finding useful sites, like one for sending your mom an electronic postcard on Mother's Day. As soon as her boyfriend decided that he was going to graduate school in Cleveland, and they determined they would move together, she got on the World Wide Web and looked up Cleveland's home page.

There Ana found access to a city map, the white pages and yellow pages, and the following links: business, city guides, community, education, entertainment and arts, events, government, health, Internet services, lodging, maps and views, news and media, real estate, recreation and sports, transportation, and travel. Ana looked up "business" and found thirty-two links to specific businesses in the Cleveland area. She also used the Yahoo! search engine, typed in the keywords "jobs" and "Cleveland," and found the classified ad listings. None of this information exactly fit with the strategy she had developed to talk to people in Cleveland who could give her advice, but she learned a great deal about the area and the range of jobs that were offered.

One last thing Ana checked was the career services office at the college she had attended. As an alumna, she was entitled to use any of the services they offered. They had their alumni directory available in CD-ROM format, with information organized by geographical location and occupation as well as alphabetically. (She decided to wait before ordering it because she was on a tight budget.) The career services office also directed her to a number of on-line job listing services and résumé databases as well as a subscription networking database. She was happy to learn that there were other resources to tap into if her contacts didn't work out.

Sam had never used a computer to access the Internet. In fact, he'd never really used a computer. When he was at the public library, he asked the reference librarian to help him get on the Internet and look up job and career information on the World Wide Web. She showed him how to use the Yahoo! search engine to get to its Career Mosaic Web site. He typed in the word "careers" and found fifty-five categories with that term. He selected "Business and Economy: Employment: Careers" and clicked on the entry. His click gave him links to sixty-six specific careers.

By this time Sam was getting overwhelmed with the amount of information available on-line. For example, he highlighted "automotive" as a specific career; clicking on this entry brought up "Auto Town" and "Car Dealerships." He clicked on "Auto Town," which brought up "Employment Office," "Information," and "Résumé Database." He chose "Employment Office" and received a listing of specific job openings.

Each step of the way, Sam was presented with choices to make in order to narrow his focus until he got the information that he wanted. He could have searched on the three words—"careers," "automotive," and "employment"—and gotten there more directly, but he may have missed valuable information along the way, like a choice for "trends in automotive careers."

Because Sam did not find any job listings that looked interesting to him, he decided to search on the keywords for the trade organizations that he had found in the printed material to get more information and investigate whether they had publications he could order. This time he used the Lycos search engine and typed in "trade associations" and then "service stations," but the only entry he found was the New York Service Station and Repair Shop Association. He decided that his best information had come from the written material. But he was happy to have learned about the Internet, as it might be useful to him in other ways.

Paula had access to the Internet from her office computer and from her personal computer at home, so she was accustomed to searching for information on the World Wide Web. She decided to see what the job listings in her area were for senior financial analysts and to investigate the salary ranges for someone in her position so that she would have some negotiating information.

She started in Yahoo! on the Career Mosaic site, clicked on the "J.O.B.S. Database," and typed in "financial analyst." She found a complete listing of jobs for financial analysts, starting with those posted most recently. There were 320 entries, each with the date of posting, name of the company, position title, and location. She clicked on one and got a screen with the company name and logo, job title, location, complete job description, phone and fax numbers, and e-mail address. It also included a job hot-line phone number and links to an on-line response form and the company home page.

She went backward one screen (by clicking on "back" at the top of the screen) and used the form provided "to conduct a more refined search," by delineating: job description, job title, company, city, and maximum number of jobs to return. She typed in "senior financial analyst" for job title and "Connecticut" for location (she wasn't looking for a particular city, so she typed in her home state), then left the rest blank. This time the search returned eleven entries, all in Connecticut, and she was able to click on each one for more information. She was happy to find out that there were a number of jobs in her area that seemed to suit her qualifications. Even though she didn't particularly want to leave her present company, she was eager to learn about her marketability. She felt that knowing other possibilities existed would give her a new perspective.

Paula also wanted some information about the value of someone with her skills. Again, she began in Yahoo! and went to the Career Mosaic site. She typed in "careers" and from that site went to "Education: Guidance: Career and Employment Planning." From there she went to "Quintessential Career and Job-Hunting Resources Guide" and clicked on "Lots of Links" to get to a review of other job-related links.

She chose "The Riley Guide: Employment Opportunities and Job Resources on the Internet" because she'd read an article in the business section of her local newspaper that rated it as one of the best job-related sites. From the home page she selected "Research for Career and Work Options" and from there "What Am I Worth?"

She was delighted with her find. Listed at this site were links to salary surveys, government wage surveys, articles on salary negotiation, and other ideas and resources. The salary surveys link brought her to choices of "Abbott, Langer, and Associates" and "Management Solutions, Inc." Clicking on "Abbott, Langer" gave her information on ordering complete salary surveys of any type. Clicking on "Management Solutions" gave her an idea of West Coast salaries listed by education, experience, and company type and size.

The last site that Paula checked was the Department of Labor home page, with links to labor market information by state. She also checked the Bureau of Labor Statistics and the U.S. Census Bureau home pages for links to information related to the labor market in Connecticut. On the whole, she felt that in two hours she'd gotten information that would help her narrow the focus of her job to take advantage of her special expertise and to negotiate a better salary and more reasonable hours.

Lamarr had just learned to use e-mail on his home computer. He had usually used the computer just for word processing. One of his daughters stopped by and taught him how to use the Internet to access the World Wide Web, and he was hooked. He decided to use the Alta Vista search engine and conducted a search using the keyword "trains." This resulted in matches with 41 categories and 1,154 site matches. So he tried "model railroads" and narrowed it down to matches with 10 categories and 318 sites. Luckily, the entries are arranged by how closely they match the keyword(s), so the first seven entries were about "hobbies: model railroading." He read through them and found information on the National Model Railroad Association: becoming a member, officers, purpose, constitution, history, and publications. He filled out the membership form on-line and downloaded the current bulletin. (All he had to do was click on "file" at the top of his browser screen and choose "save as," then name the file and select where he wanted to save it on his hard drive.) He bookmarked all of these sites so he could return to them directly whenever he wanted.

Lamarr was most excited about the potential of making contact with others who shared his passion for model trains. All of the sites for the association included e-mail addresses of contact people. He was going to search next for a newsgroup or discussion list, then later maybe find a chat room. He even found the Model Railroad Trader Weboard, where he could see what trains were available in trade. His problem now was finding time on the Web and time with his trains, all in the evenings after work.

▪ ENJOY EXPLORING! ▪

This is a brief journey through the variety of possibilities that exist for you in the world of the Internet. It's most important first to learn the process of searching for on-line information so you can keep up with the rapid changes in technology and in newsgroups, discussion lists, and Web sites. Don't be dismayed by the amount of information on-line. Just jump in and start searching. You'll be amazed at what you find and delighted at how quickly you learn to take advantage of the wealth of electronic resources.

thirteen

Networks

It's difficult to talk about time in relation to networks. We recommend that building a network be an ongoing and lifelong activity. That doesn't mean handing out your business card indiscriminately wherever you go. As you know by now, we have a strong philosophy about working with meaning. Well, the same goes for networking—do it continually, but do it with meaning.

Networking doesn't have to be about wearing a suit, drinking mineral water, and turning on the charm. Establishing networks of contacts who may be able to help you in your career can be as natural as joining a group of neighbors working on a neighborhood issue or as formal as signing on with a career advising group through your college alumni association. The point is to meet a variety of people and establish a genuine connection based on shared interests so that, in time, you feel as comfortable asking for job-related advice as you do asking for gardening tips. Never underestimate the ability of a friend or acquaintance to introduce you to the person or situation that will help you along your career path.

For example, Rosa found herself newly divorced at forty, never having gone to college or had a job outside of raising her family. Through another Girl Scout mom, she heard that a small company operating out of a neighborhood garage was looking for someone to answer phones and do general receptionist duties. Rosa's interpersonal skills and the organizational abilities she'd developed as the mother of three daughters helped her get the job. Her skills grew with the company. Now, fifteen years later, she's vice-president in the new East Coast regional office. She's never forgotten how she started her career with a mom-to-mom connection.

▪ WHERE CAN YOU NETWORK? ▪

Schools

Whether you are a high school graduate or went on to complete college or a professional school program, your alma mater is a good place to make contacts. Attend your high school reunion and find out what your classmates are doing. You can learn a great deal of information about careers from listening to others tell tales of their work life. Don't just talk to your old friends; talk to the boy who was your physics lab partner or the girl who sat next to you in algebra—they may be doing something fascinating with their careers.

Technical and professional schools and colleges and universities all have career advisers and job placement offices. If you are a student, be sure to take advantage of their career services. If you are a graduate of the institution, you can usually continue to use the job listings and résumé service.

Most postsecondary schools also have alumni groups that offer a variety of career and placement services. In fact, this is a growing area. Your alumni association may have some system of alumni contacts, people who will talk to you about the work they do and serve as career consultants. It's becoming common to make available a computerized database of alumni contacts. An advantage of making contact with a graduate of the same institution is that you share a personal, familiar connection. A shared loyalty can provide an important link to busy people because it establishes some credibility at the outset. In addition, you know that because the contact is willing to be a part of the program, he or she will make time to see you and will have good feelings about being asked for help. What more do you need?

Professional Associations

Professional development courses or workshops offer the perfect opportunity to meet people who share your interests. These may be offered by a company specializing in training or by a professional association. If you are already working in a specific field, make sure you join one of your professional associations. Membership can provide a wealth of information, from listings for continuing education to position announcements. If another field interests you, the professional association representing that area can be a gold mine of information. All associations maintain a directory of their members, a good place to develop contacts for your network.

If you're a student, it's possible that the professional association in your area of interest offers a discount on student memberships. Check with one of your professors for information. If you're already working in a specific type of business or industry, ask your colleagues about the professional association that represents their interests and send for information. You usually don't have to join just to get information or to attend a conference. As we pointed out in Chapter 11, you can always go to the library and look in the *Encyclopedia of Associations* or the *National Trade and Professional Associations of the United States* for references to groups in your area of interest and send for general information about the occupation. There's a trade or professional association for every topic you can imagine, from the American Soybean Association to the Wood Heating Alliance.

Community

Getting involved in local community activity can generate other networks. Whether you're donating time to a community foundation or a neighborhood association, take advantage of getting to know the other volunteers. The same holds true for social clubs and special interest groups, like a ski club or a softball team. Religious affiliations also yield a source of contacts, particularly if you're an active member.

Here again we want to make a basic point: do something that's important to you or that you truly love, and you're sure to meet other people who will be good professional contacts. And it's not a one-way street; you'll be a resource to others as you get to know them.

Clubs

A traditional way to build your network is through groups whose underlying purpose is specifically to make professional contacts. Business groups and service clubs fall in this category. Although the Rotary has a mission of service, it also provides members with helpful business contacts. The Business and Professional Women's Club is a similar organization, combining community service with a strong network. Membership in some of these organizations is by invitation only. If you have a special interest in a particular club, there are bound to be people in your growing network who can sponsor your membership or take you to a club function as their guest.

It's important to express genuine interest and to have a goal for your involvement with a specific organization. Don't get bogged down being a member of so many organizations that you have a huge network but no time to make sincere connections and get meaningful information.

We both subscribe to a luncheon series for business and professional women that showcases interesting speakers once a month. The forty-five-minute talks focus on a timely topic, like welfare reform, election politics, or the immigration and naturalization system. It's a perfect venue for very busy women to meet, talk, eat lunch, hear an interesting speaker, and get back to work, all within two hours. Most of us are short on time, but we all recognize that the women in the group form a valuable resource pool. The keys to making this a success are a wide variety but a limited number of women subscribers and a chart that has everyone sitting with someone different at each luncheon. Perfect networking!

▪ HOW JOB SEEKERS USE NETWORKS ▪

When Ana first decided to move to Cleveland, she panicked because she didn't know anyone there. Then she remembered a friend from college who had grown up in Cleveland and whose parents still lived there. She called Brian and asked for names of contacts in the Cleveland area. He said that he was sure his parents would be willing to help. He gave her their phone number and offered to let them know she'd be calling. This made it much easier for Ana to make the initial call, knowing they would have heard about her from Brian.

When she reached them a few days later, they'd been expecting her call. Ana had carefully considered how she would present herself on the phone and had noted the information she wanted to gain from them. She'd prepared questions, written them out, and practiced with her mother before making the call. She wanted to communicate enthusiasm about her move and confidence in her job skills. What she hoped for were referrals—names of people she could talk to about exploring job possibilities when she made an initial trip to Cleveland in the spring.

They talked for quite some time and shared names of friends with Ana. As lifetime residents, they were very well connected in Cleveland. But they were worried that they might not be much help, because people they knew best tended to be CEOs, directors, or presidents of their organizations, people not directly involved in hiring. Little did they know how helpful this would really be to Ana, for she was looking for *advice*, and who better to get it from than someone at the top? She would have entree into some of the most prestigious organizations in Cleveland. Though her degree was in Spanish literature, not in business or accounting or finance or law, she knew her skills and could articulate them with precision and confidence. By the time she made her first trip to Cleveland, she was poised to gather as much advice and information as possible.

Following her conversation with Brian's parents, she made a list of the names and telephone numbers they had given her. She called each number and explained to the secretary or receptionist who answered that she was writing a letter to Mr. or Ms. So-and-So and asked for the official title of the person and his or her address. She composed a letter with a brief introduction of herself, mentioning her connection to Brian's parents, and requested a fifteen-to-twenty-minute meeting on the Friday she'd be visiting Cleveland. She made it clear that she was beginning to explore career directions in Cleveland before moving there and that their advice about the community as well as their personal perspective about careers could be very helpful. She stated that she would call in about a week to make an appointment.

It took a while for Ana to convince herself that all she really wanted was advice, not a quick and easy job offer. She was worried about finding a good job and had to bear in mind that advice would lead her in the right direction and keep her in charge of her career. She placed the follow-up calls and was able to make three appointments for informational interviews.

A few weeks later Ana and her boyfriend took a three-day trip to Cleveland so that Ana could do her informational interviewing while her boyfriend looked for an apartment. Her interviews went well. She got solid advice about working in Cleveland, an introduction to a variety of workplaces, and insight about how and where someone with her skills would fit in. Her nine additional contacts gave her plenty of informational interviews to arrange prior to her move.

Although Ana was terrified and nervous before her first informational interview, she was fortified to go on when the first person she talked to gave her three more names. She used her Ah-ha résumé as a guide to talk about her skills and experience and asked for advice on how she could best apply them in the workplace. She brought with her the written set of questions she'd prepared, and she diligently took notes at every meeting. By the end of the day, she was a new woman, confident that she'd be able to continue to direct her career strategy and find a job to her liking. She was happy that she'd worn her new suit, because it really helped her to feel that she fit into the professional culture—a skirt and sweater would definitely have marked her as a neophyte.

Sam had been working for a number of years, but his connections were mostly informal. He didn't belong to a professional association and didn't have time to volunteer in the community. He and Tonya were active in the young couples' group in their church, and they enjoyed having friends and family over for dinner. Though he spent most of his free time with his family, he belonged to a bowling team that played in a league once a week. A couple of the guys on his bowling team owned small businesses, so he talked to them informally about what it was like to run a business, manage employees, prepare payrolls, and so on. They were pretty straight with him about the downside of running a business. As they said, "You may be the boss, but you're tied to it."

Beginning to worry that owning a service station may not be exactly what he wanted, he asked the pastor of his church whether there were any members of the congregation who were service station owners. The pastor gave him the name of Luis Rivera, an older man who had owned a franchise station for the past twenty years.

Sam contacted Luis and invited him out for a beer one day after work. He thought carefully in advance about what he wanted to know and asked Luis about hours, vacation, income, stability, and employee relations, as well as what it was like to own a small business. Luis seemed hesitant at first, but he warmed up and was happy to help Sam in any way he could. He loved having a business that had provided him with a decent income all these years. But lately, he'd had some problems finding good employees, and he hadn't had a vacation in the last ten years. He was always at the station to open it at 6 A.M. and close it at 10 P.M., often without a chance to go home in between. He was thinking of looking for work that would be easier on him. Owning a service station was a job for a younger man. As they talked, he wondered aloud whether Sam might be in a position to buy his business. This seemed like a stroke of luck for Sam, but he didn't have the money to invest in the business right now. He was hoping to spend a few years as a service station manager, learning the ropes while he built up his capital and his credit. But if Luis was willing, Sam would be interested in working his way into being station manager, easing Luis's load a bit and learning the business from him. This seemed like a good idea to both of them.

Paula was in a position to use the networks she'd developed through years of working in her profession, volunteering in the community, and raising her family. She was a member of a local professional association, Women in Finance, and attended the monthly meetings. Through this association, she knew many women working in her field. She made lunch dates with two of them whom she knew she could trust to be discreet, so she could ask them for advice on her career possibilities. Paula was also on the volunteer board of advisers for one of the local homeless shelters. She was able to get some informal information on executive recruiters from another board member who managed hiring for a local firm. She talked with the other mothers at her daughter's swim meet to find out how they balanced their work and family life, and she got some good insight from a few of the women. One worked in marketing for a major firm and was able to manage her hours by developing a specialty area and concentrating on the clients in that area.

As Paula continued to gain more information, she began to realize that all of her associations with people provided potential networking opportunities, that the key was to ask very specific questions and listen carefully to the answers. At the same time, she knew that professional decorum forced her to be mindful of the information she revealed with respect to her company and her position.

Years ago, when Lamarr first became fascinated with model trains, he started a newsletter about model railroading. The newsletter lasted only a few years, but he remained in touch with a few of the people he met through that venture. He decided to let them know that within the next few years he would be retiring from his "day job" and to ask for their suggestions for new directions. Could a newsletter succeed if he devoted all his time to it? Was there a need for another model railroading newsletter? What about his train collection? Would there be interest in an antique dealer who specialized in model trains? He couldn't talk to his neighbors or his friends about this, but he could certainly contact other people with similar interests. He wrote letters and made phone calls to everyone he remembered from the old newsletter days, and he gleaned valuable advice from each of them. Even though Lamarr was not the gregarious type, he had enough contacts to begin to generate a network of people with a similar interest in model trains to give him feedback about his ideas for the future.

What's your network like? How many possibilities are radiating from the quadrants of your LifeCircle? Keep in mind that aimless networking is just that—aimless. Make sincere connections with people and make them purposeful, for life and for work. Remember your objectives. Remember it's *what's what* and not *who's who* that counts. And remember that networking means helping others, too.

fourteen

Career Services

Career services are often seen as a way to save time getting a job. Just go to an agency, talk to a placement counselor, or look through the list of openings, and you're all set. Well, not really. There are no shortcuts to finding your best work. Spend the bulk of your time doing your own thinking and planning, and you can minimize the time someone else has to think for you.

There are many types of career services, ranging from temporary agencies where you can get a placement free of charge to executive career counseling agencies where you might pay thousands of dollars for career advice. The important thing to remember when considering using some type of career service is to stay in charge of your career. Do not hand over decision-making to someone else, even a career professional. By the time you get to this chapter, you should know your skills and job preferences better than anyone else, and you should be able to communicate them to a professional who can assist you in locating resources.

▪ WHAT CAREER SERVICES ARE OUT THERE? ▪

Job Assessment Center

If you still feel you need help identifying your job interests, you may want to seek out the services of a reputable job testing center. Most offer tools such as the Strong Interest Inventory or the Myers-Briggs Personality Type Indicator, measures that can provide information on work preferences. Just make sure that you're not expecting someone else to decide what kind of job would make you happy. Regard test results with caution and interpret for yourself how the information would be most useful.

Career Counseling

A career counselor will be able to give you advice and assistance on your career but will not guarantee a job placement. It's important to be selective when choosing a career counselor, because you're purchasing a service that varies with the expertise of the individual. Check references and reputation carefully. You can expect solid advice on résumé writing, interviewing, and negotiating a job offer from a reputable career counselor. Beware of anyone who promises immediate success for a high fee.

School Career Services

Technical and trade schools and colleges and universities all have career advisers and job placement offices. If you're a student, be sure to take advantage of your institution's career services. If you're a graduate of the institution, you can usually continue to use the job listings and résumé service. No degree comes with the guarantee of a job, but postsecondary institutions are becoming more committed to helping their graduates think about career exploration, and many offer assistance to those in career transitions.

Temporary Agencies

Temporary help agencies may be the place to turn if you need to earn money quickly while continuing your job search. Register with agencies that specialize in placing people with your skills and qualifications. Approach each temporary placement that you accept with a skill-building attitude. Some temporary positions may turn into permanent placement, so take the opportunity to consider whether you would choose this line of work for a career. At the very least, you can build your skill base and perhaps even make an impression that will net you an outstanding reference.

Employment Agencies

Employment agencies are another potential resource in your job search. Some are privately owned, for-profit businesses, and others are run by nonprofit governmental offices. They may offer some services that are similar to career counselors, but their primary goal is to link you with job openings, not to do vocational counseling.

Private Agencies. Private employment agencies can be individually owned or part of a national franchise. It is important to check them out very carefully so that you can be sure they're reputable. A particularly good sign is a business with membership in the *National Association of Personnel Consultants* or staff members who have *Certified Personnel Consultant* status. You're under no obligation until you sign a contract. Don't sign any document that obliges you to pay a fee unless you feel certain that your needs will be met in a professional fashion. Again, beware of anyone who promises immediate success for a high fee—they may be more interested in getting your money than in helping you find a job.

Government Agencies. Local and state governments have employment services that will send out your résumé to employers who have positions registered with them. They maintain local and national job listings, although they may not be the place to find the most recent postings.

What can they do for you? Take our area—Madison, Wisconsin—as an example. The City of Madison Human Resources Department posts city government job openings. The Dane County Department of Employee Relations Job Center offers job search assistance, help with career exploration, and information on financial and medical assistance with no fee to employers or applicants. The State of Wisconsin's Department of Workforce Development, Division of Workforce Excellence, Job Center Bureau maintains statewide and nationwide listings in all occupational areas with no fee to employers or applicants. A job seeker can even register to receive the biweekly job postings by mail for a small fee.

Every state will have employment services, but their offerings may differ, as will access. Maybe your county and/or city also provide employment services. Your reference librarian will be able to fill you in on exactly what's available where you live.

The federal government has agencies all over the United States, such as the United Migrant Opportunity Services and Veterans' Affairs Regional Offices. Many will have job information available. You can also call the Federal Information Service at (800) 688-9889 to get access to general information concerning the federal government. The Office of Personnel Management's Career America Connection is available at (912) 757-3000 for more specific job information, or you can contact the closest office of your state employment service.

Outplacement Services

Outplacement services are usually contracted for by a company that's downsizing, or they may be offered as part of a severance package for a departing employee. The goal of outplacement is to find employees—generally executive-level—a placement outside the present situation, hence the term "outplacement." If you want to rethink your career path instead of going into a position similar to your most recent one, then you will want to develop your own career search strategies in addition to using outplacement services.

Executive Recruiters

Executive recruiters may be individual contractors or may work for an executive recruitment firm. They are paid by employers to find people with executive-level skills to fit a specific position opening. In a tight applicant market they may also represent people with midlevel skills. Executive recruiters are not in the business of helping unemployed workers find jobs. They help companies fill critical positions.

If you fit the profile of a desirable executive-level employee, an executive recruiter will keep your résumé on file and will contact you if and when you match with an employer's request. If you have a record of achievement at an executive level and you want to investigate a job change or advancement, then it may be to your benefit to talk with an executive recruiter. If you're actually negotiating a job change, it's prudent not to reveal any of your pending possibilities to executive recruiters. If you disclose such information, recruiters may take the opportunity to introduce unwanted competition from their files.

▪ HOW JOB SEEKERS USE CAREER SERVICES ▪

Ana wanted to take some time looking for what she called a career job, as opposed to a minimum-wage job, once she moved to Cleveland. She allowed herself four weeks to do informational interviewing and narrow her focus enough to actually locate a position. If she hadn't found a job within that time, she would contact a temporary help agency and try to negotiate a twenty-five-to-thirty-hour per week position so she'd have some income while she continued her job search.

In the middle of her fourth week, she had a crisis of confidence and decided she really needed to be working. She called three temporary placement agencies that she knew handled professional-level positions. She made appointments to take their employment tests (such as word processing and writing) and registered her interests with them. They had immediate openings for her at more than minimum wage and would even offer benefits after a certain number of months with the company.

She took a job as an executive assistant to a vice-president at the corporate headquarters of a national retail company. Unfortunately, she did not have the choice to work less than a forty-hour week, so she had to carry on her job search by making telephone contacts during her breaks, and appointments over her lunch hour. She was determined not to give up the ground she'd gained in seeking a real "career job."

Sam visited the state employment agency to check on jobs for automotive mechanics. He thought that he'd see whether there were positions in this area that might allow him to work his way up to management with a state agency. For example, if he were to work in a city, county, or state shop that maintains government vehicles and maybe take some management courses at the local community college in the evenings, eventually he could be in a good position for promotion. Maybe this would be one way to satisfy his desire to get ahead, without actually having to put up the capital to buy a service station. He was still in an exploratory stage, so he wanted to look into all the possibilities.

Unfortunately, he had to take an hour off from his current job to go to the local Job Center first thing one morning. He was impressed with the range of services offered by the Job Center and wished he had time to take one of the interviewing or résumé or Internet workshops. In that hour, however, he was able to do a computer search of all job listings for auto mechanics in public agencies and get a printout of the ones that sounded interesting. Each printout gave details about how to get an application and whom to call for further information. He decided to follow up by calling to ask about opportunities for promotion and career development before asking for any applications. In this way, he could find out whether it was possible to get the type of job he wanted working for a government agency and develop his career at the same time. After all, government agencies usually have good pension plans and early retirement options. He was learning to look at every part of his Lifeline.

Paula decided to call a headhunter, also known in polite circles as an executive recruiter. She was intent on learning her true market value. She'd become very curious about whether she might find a company she liked just as much as her current employer but with a more flexible position for her. She first looked under "executive search consultants" in the yellow pages of her local telephone directory. Listed were a number of local consultants as well as national recruiting firms representing general and specialized areas, such as sales and technical work.

She recognized some of the names from hearing the managers in her company talk about them. She avoided people who typically sent unqualified candidates, and she discreetly checked with friends on the reputation of others. Based on what she learned, she selected a firm with national stature and called for an appointment to meet a particular staff recruiter who worked with other firms in the financial industry. (He'd represented one of her close friends who had moved on to another company and who had described him as straightforward and very professional.) The recruiter asked her to send a current résumé and offered to meet with her in a week. Before she went she made sure that this person and the firm he worked for were listed in one of the books she had checked out from the library—either *The Directory of Executive Recruiters* or *The Guide to Executive Recruiters*. Although a listing didn't guarantee quality of service, it at least guaranteed credibility in the field.

Paula was eager to share information about her skills and work history and get a realistic picture of her market value. She communicated this to the recruiter at the interview and was surprised to learn that her current salary was at the midpoint for someone with her qualifications. The recruiter told her of one immediate opening for a senior financial analyst, but it was a position very similar to the one Paula already had, with long hours and midlevel pay. She explained to the recruiter that she wanted to stay in the same geographical location, and he promised to let her know about any appropriate positions as they came up.

Lamarr's course of action was to consult a career counselor. Concerned that he wouldn't be able to make any money on his model train hobby, he wanted to get some other ideas on retirement careers, based on the skills he'd perfected all these years on the job. He wasn't sure if any of these skills were transferable to another type of occupation suitable for a slower-paced lifestyle. He was willing to pay for a few sessions to get some vocational counseling, and maybe even take one of those aptitude tests. He was interested in exploring all avenues of possibilities for change and was eager to get an expert opinion.

He looked in the yellow pages under "career and vocational counseling" and found individuals with backgrounds in social work as well as some who were clinical psychologists. A number of career counseling firms were also listed. He chose a firm that employed licensed clinical psychologists who were experienced in administering and interpreting assessments, helping clients explore career choices and opportunities, and doing job-focused counseling. He made this choice because since his heart attack he'd been thinking of seeking counseling to help him manage the stress of his job. Maybe he could get some advice on stress reduction at the same time that he was investigating retirement career possibilities.

Career services can be a great help, particularly if you know what information you're seeking. And that's the key—you're seeking *information*, not *answers*. Only you can determine what will be your best work. And the right information will help you make that choice.

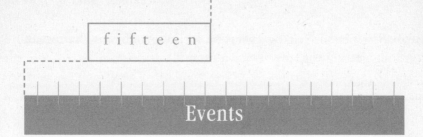

fifteen

Events

You can spend an hour or a day or a weekend at a job fair or career forum. The time matters less than your preparation. What's important is to have some objectives and a strategy outlined in advance and decide how much time you want to devote to a particular event.

For example, we recently went to a career forum to make contact with human resource professionals. We each spoke with a dozen people in an hour. We had decided our strategy in advance and went prepared with a list of questions. We had budgeted only an hour, so we wanted to use the time wisely. We met our goal and learned more about current recruiting and hiring efforts.

Decide on your strategy and your time limit prior to each event you attend and go prepared. If you have all day, relax and enjoy meeting and talking to people. If you have only your lunch hour, decide in advance what your objective is and whom you want to meet.

Job- or career-related events can range from a neighborhood mentoring lunch at the local deli to a community-wide job fair extravaganza. A few years ago, a small group of men and women in our neighborhood who work independently at home decided to meet to offer support to one of the neighbors who was contemplating a drastic career change. The mentoring benefit felt by everyone in the group was the impetus to continue getting together twice a month.

▪ WHAT'S GOING ON OUT THERE FOR YOU? ▪

Mentoring

Mentoring has become a buzzword in the workplace. It is not a fad, but an integral part of developing our best work, as more and more people recognize that we can all benefit from mentoring throughout our lives. What exactly do we mean by the word "mentor?" The dictionary definition is "wise and trusted counselor," but the word comes from Greek literature and originally meant "adviser." Modern definitions are based on descriptions of the role of a mentor: communicator, counselor, coach, adviser, broker, referral agent, and advocate. To be a good mentor requires a blend of sincere interest in a person's welfare and a certain level of objectivity.

Informal mentoring has occurred in the workplace for a long time, but as diversity increases, it has become important to establish more formal mentoring programs, particularly for women and ethnic minorities. Professional associations, alumni organizations, and community centers are some of the groups that may offer mentoring programs. Take advantage of these programs to meet people and ask for advice on your career.

Conventions

Professional conferences and trade conventions provide excellent opportunities to meet people in your area of career interest. Use the breaks to introduce yourself, especially to the speaker, if there is one. You can develop important and lasting contacts and even establish friendships over time. In addition, these events usually have job postings and a mechanism for connecting job seekers with potential employers. Even if you're not interviewing for a particular job, it's helpful to meet the interviewers and ask their advice on the skills employers in that field are seeking. If you request a fifteen-minute meeting and are prepared with specific questions, an interviewer is likely to accommodate you in a busy schedule.

Workshops

Seminars and workshops with a special focus on job search skills can be helpful if you need encouragement. Those offered by for-profit companies are usually advertised in the business section of the local newspaper. You may be able to find similar information presented free of charge through workshops at the local Job Center. In either case, it's important for you to take in the information with the attitude of maintaining control of your career and not giving over the decision-making to someone else.

Job Fairs

Job fairs are sponsored by a group of businesses and by local employment agencies and sometimes by companies recruiting a group of new employees. Take the opportunity to gather information on company backgrounds, job descriptions, and hiring procedures. Job fairs are announced in local newspapers and on the radio and thus tend to be crowded affairs. Enjoy the energy, but don't expect to get personal attention, though you should be prepared (in image and information) to meet someone who could be your potential boss. Think beforehand about what you want to learn and go to a career fair on an information-seeking mission. After you've attended, see how the information adds to your strategic search or suggests new directions to explore through informational interviews.

Career Forums

A career forum is a bit different from a job fair, because it's usually sponsored by an educational institution. These events range from talks by people in local businesses and trades to elaborate booths set up by large corporations. Often forums are organized primarily for students, but alumni are usually welcome. Ask the career advising office to put you on the mailing list for your school, whether high school, technical school, or college, and you'll get the announcements in the mail. Career forums present a wonderful opportunity to meet people from a variety of organizations, ask questions about their line of work and their particular company, and get some feedback on the value of someone with your skills.

Approach a career forum with a goal of talking to as many people as possible: make contact, get information, collect written material and business cards, and leave your own business card. Follow up with a phone call within the next week to get more specific information; if the company sounds interesting and is hiring people like you, ask to whom you should send your résumé. If you don't have a business card, or if you prefer to use one without your present employment logo, you can have an inexpensive one printed with your name, home address, and telephone number. It's important to have a card to give to the people you meet, because it will help them get in touch with you in the future.

▪ HOW JOB SEEKERS USE EVENTS ▪

Ana read in the *Cleveland Plain Dealer* about a job fair to be held at the local convention center, sponsored by the city employment bureau in conjunction with a number of local businesses. Even though she'd been enmeshed in doing informational interviews almost continuously since her move, she decided to take a day and broaden her scope. She had some business cards printed with her name and her new address and phone number, put on her suit, grabbed a pen and a pad of paper, and went off to seek new kinds of information. At the very least, she could get an idea of the range of employers in the Cleveland area.

She found that many of the employers represented were looking for unskilled, entry-level workers. However, she was able to learn about a wide array of organizations and talk to some of the recruiters about opportunities for someone with her level of skills and a college degree. She gathered business cards and written materials from organizations that interested her and left her card in return. In each case, she was also able to find out the name of an appropriate person to contact for follow-up.

Sam received an announcement in the mail about an upcoming career forum at the technical school where he'd studied auto mechanics. He was working in his chosen career, so he didn't think the forum would be of much use to him, but he decided to check it out anyway. He went early so that he could meet some of the people before the onslaught of students arrived. He talked to a number of people who were representing automotive businesses—auto parts shops, convenience store/service station franchises, manufacturer's representatives for automotive supplies. He also attended a special talk on starting a small business and one on purchasing a franchise. By the end of the evening, he'd amassed a wealth of new information that would help him think about his future plans, and he'd made contacts for further exploration.

Paula attended the regional conference of Women in Finance, the professional association in which she had been active for many years. She was interested in many of the presentations, but she concentrated on talking to other women she felt would be able to offer her some good career advice. She had thought about it beforehand and jotted down the names of women she wanted to be sure to run into. She arrived early at the conference so she'd have a chance to network during the registration period. That was the place to catch people to talk for a few minutes or make a plan for meeting later. As it turned out, she missed most of the presentations. But she talked to a lot of women and listened very carefully to their advice, taking notes whenever she could. Paula's history with the organization had made others aware of her professionalism and integrity, and several said that they were thrilled to be asked for advice.

Paula was particularly fascinated by the story of a woman who said her company offered a structured mentoring program and that her mentor had helped her refashion her job after the birth of her son. She had continued to be promoted within the organization, but on a career path that was more manageable during the years that her son was young. Now that he was grown, she was devoting more time to expanding her career and creating new opportunities within her company. She'd recently written a proposal to institute an innovative financial service and had gotten the go-ahead from her superiors. What an exciting mentor she could be for Paula! They agreed to meet again.

Lamarr had attended a local meeting of a model railroading group many years earlier when he was attempting to start his newsletter. He hadn't gone in recent years because he was concentrating on building up his train collection and he enjoyed his hobby in a solitary fashion. Now, he thought, maybe it was time to start becoming active in a local chapter of the National Model Railroad Association or at least to attend the national yearly convention and find out whether others were making a living from their hobby. He'd written for information about the convention, which was to be held in the spring at the Indianapolis Convention Center. He decided to take a few vacation days and go. He spent time carefully planning objectives for what he wanted to learn at the convention and thinking about the connections he wanted to make.

When he arrived, he was delighted to learn that there were also exhibitors—dealers in antique model trains and book publishers looking for new authors. He spent a great deal of his time talking with these people and started to formulate some ideas about perhaps being able to get involved in dealing antique model trains on the Internet. After all, he was enamored with the possibilities of on-line commercial activity; he didn't want to set up a retail shop; yet he was passionate about working with his vast model train collection. He had lunches with two dealers to ask questions about their businesses, and he had lengthy conversations with convention attendees to discern interest in on-line model train sales and exchanges. He talked to the publishers to test their level of interest in a model train book he'd been writing for years and learned that he probably wouldn't be able to develop a retirement income just from writing. But they encouraged him to stay in touch. If he wanted to fund his writing, he would have to find another way, yet he also needed to make more time for his writing, something he truly enjoyed and wanted to expand in his retirement. More and more, the on-line model train dealing idea sounded like it might work.

All of our characters defined their objectives before attending an event. Consequently, they were able to make good use of their time. Choose your events wisely and target the information you want to gather. Then you can make a habit of choosing events that contribute to developing the best work of your life.

Epilogue to Part 3

We left Ana, Sam, Paula, and Lamarr in the middle of their career search, and we thought you might like to know what decisions each of them made. Because they're based on real characters, we can tell you what they're doing today.

Remember that Ana took a temp job four weeks after moving to Cleveland. Through her informational interviews, she narrowed her interest down to two organizations—a large university and a museum. She garnered the respect and admiration of her primary contacts in both places and through them was able to meet a number of other administrators in key positions. She had an interview for a position at the university and one at the museum, but neither looked promising. The university was also interviewing internal candidates, and the museum was interviewing someone who'd held the same position in another cultural center. So she decided to cut her losses (and lower her stress about money) and take the temp job while she continued to arrange informational interviews during her lunch hour. She continued to expand her network by calling people whose names she'd been given casually before her move.

Two days into her temp job, she got a call from the university offering her the position she'd interviewed for. The next day she got a call from the museum saying they'd hired the other candidate but they had another position to offer

Ana. Everyone at the museum had been impressed with her self-presentation, and they wanted to find a position for her. Ana was thrilled, and pleased that she'd initiated these opportunities through networking. She returned to both places for additional interviews.

Ana has now been working happily at the university for the past year and is enjoying a new sense of power and control over her career choices. She is committed to continuing her career development by directing it herself.

Sam enjoyed working for Luis and learning the ins and outs of owning a service station. He was a good station manager, and Luis could rely on Sam to handle any aspect of the business. Sam was at the station day and night, yet he still found time to read the trade publications on service stations and talk to other business owners. He even went to some workshops at the local Small Business Development Center to learn about up-to-date business practices.

He loved the customers and he had great respect for Luis, but he was surprised by the amount of time it took to run the business end of the station. Payroll, orders, supplies, vendors, advertising, overhead, and on and on. He hadn't realized there was so much time spent in office work. It seemed that the more successful the business was, the less time he had with customers or their cars. He was having doubts about wanting to be the boss, so he finally confided in Luis. Luckily, Luis took his role as a mentor very seriously. He was honest with Sam about the difficulties he had with his family because he was rarely home. He knew that Sam would be great at taking over the station, but he just couldn't recommend it, knowing Sam's values concerning his family.

So what did Sam do? Well, he'd learned so much about his strengths and values and the way he preferred to work that he decided to pursue his dream of being his own boss. He rented a small garage in the urban business area near his house and repaired cars on his own. He was the boss, but he had no employees to worry about. He would drive to a customer's home or office, leave his car and pick up their car, drive it to his garage, do the repairs, and drive it back. If the car wouldn't start, he'd work on it where it was. We hear that his customers love him and they've been eager to spread the word. He takes care of the cars for most of the employees in a large office building. They call and make arrangements; then, when they get out of work, their car is fixed. And Sam only works during the day, so he's home in the evening and on weekends with his family. He has continued to use the Internet to stay on top of information in the automotive industry, and he is active in his regional service station and repair shop association.

Paula found out that someone with her skills was very valuable on the job market. She also found out that there were other jobs out there for her. But she decided it was worth a try to follow in the steps of the woman who'd become her mentor. So she wrote a proposal to her company to manage one small segment of their financial business: with her skills and ideas she predicted she could grow that segment by a significant amount. It would take hard work, and it meant she'd be on the line to produce, but it also meant no more traveling and fewer extended workdays.

Paula implemented her ideas, which streamlined the processing system of an important financial segment and increased profits considerably. She won the complete support of her company as her proposal became a reality. Paula now has a manageable work schedule, time with her children, and time with her parents. She hasn't reached her productivity goal yet, but she's well on her way. And the top managers in her company continue to be astounded by her vision and her initiatives.

Though a solitary fellow, Lamarr really started to shine as he got more and more into communicating with other model train buffs. He had his collection appraised and found that he was sitting on a gold mine. While not comfortable opening up an antique model train shop or even engaging in actively selling face-to-face, Lamarr found that an on-line business was just right for him.

Lamarr retired last winter and now trades in antique model trains over the Internet almost daily. He sells from his collection and brokers sales for other collectors. He has a very popular Web site and is doing a brisk business. He's thinking about creating an on-line newsletter about antique model trains, perhaps even selling advertising and subscriptions. He reports that his life is much less stressful—and he even has time to take a daily walk and watch his diet. He says he's never felt better. Lamarr's interests and skills have been refashioned to fit his life stage. He never dreamed he'd be able to work with so much satisfaction and balance.

These four people are doing the best work of their lives. Ana, because she has learned the power of making her own career choices. Sam, because he decided on the priorities in his life and stuck to them. Paula, because she achieved the balance she sought. And Lamarr, because he's making an income from doing what he loves most. You, too, can do the best work of your life—through Clarity, Strategy, and Action.

Your best work will be marked by eagerness and enthusiasm. You won't have to guess whether you've found it, you'll know. More important, the work you do in the future will be based on clarity about yourself, strategies you've determined, and actions you've planned. The sense of ownership and control you'll feel will bring depth and stability to the sheer pleasure of doing work you enjoy.

Go back through the book and review the exercises at the end of each chapter. Add to the pile of paper that is your Ah-ha résumé in progress. Be generous and thorough in reviewing your past. Dig things up. Be affectionate, too. Remember all the good things you are and have done.

Continue to see your world—your LifeCircle—as a place of abundance. Continually look for opportunities that resonate with your strengths, skills, and values. As you explore possible actions, be respectful of your time and resources. Keep in mind that there's no such thing as five years from now when it comes to moving toward a goal.

Start the best work of your life today by establishing and meeting your highest standards in at least some aspect of your life. Once you attain that quality, consider how it will feel as you expand your greatest expectations to all the ways you work. Soon you'll be able to trim away what is mediocre, driven by others' expectations, or simply habitual and irrelevant. What will remain will be you at your best.

We're all entitled to do our best work because, as human beings, our job is to fulfill our highest potential. Help others learn what you learn. Teaching and mentoring are good ways to stay honest with ourselves.

As you strive to find and do the best work of your life, remember that the striving is a constant process and the only way to hold on to your *best*. Your vision for the future will be based on:

The linear view of your Lifeline—past to future
The sweeping view of your LifeCircle—an abundant present
The focused view of all that you need to know—
                    Clarity
                    Strategy
                    Action

Index

Achievements, 47–52
  best work versus jobs, 52
  outside workplace, 48
  and personal talents, 49
  and qualifications, 54–55
  reasons for reflection on,
    50–52
  in résumé, 84–91, 94–95,
    97–98
  work-related, 48–49
Action, meaning of, 2
Action steps
  for establishing integrity
    and identity, 177–178
  forming vision, 27–28
  for networking, 120
  for opportunity tracking,
    140–141
  reconstructing personal
    history, 43–44
  résumé creation, 103–105
  for strategy initiation,
    165–166
  taking control of career,
    78
  understanding work history,
    60
Advocacy, 122

Alea, Patricia V., 229–230
Alta Vista, 200
America Online, 192
Appearance
  for informational/referral
    interviews, 128
  for job interview, 139
Attitude, and job interview,
    138–139
Awards, résumé, 97–98

Balance,
  LifeCircle for, 75–78
  maintaining balance, 22–23
Bookmarking sites, Internet,
    194, 198
Bookstore, for job search
    information, 185
BusinessWeek, 188

Career America Connection,
    212
Career changes, average
    number of, 20

Career counseling, 210
Career forums, 219–220
Career Mosaic Web site, 197, 198,
    199
Career path, 57–58
    with random pattern, 57
    self-directed path, 57–58
Career services, 209–216
    career counseling, 210
    employment agencies, 211
    executive recruiters,
        212–213
    government agencies,
        211–212
    guidelines for use, 213–216
    job assessment centers, 210
    on-line career centers, 194
    outplacement services, 212
    school career services, 210
    temporary agencies, 211
Careertalk, 230
Certified Personnel Consultant,
    211
Clarity
    and goals, 23
    meaning of, 2
    and vision, 24–26
Clubs, and networking, 204
Communication skills
    forms of, 93
    in résumé, 94–95, 99
Community
    and networking, 203–204
    networking in, 115, 118
Comprehensive Internet Reference
    to Discussion Lists, 196
CompuServe, 192
Contingency employment,
    145
Conventions, and job search,
    218–219
Counseling, career counseling,
    210
Creative types, networking with,
    116, 118

Decision-making
    and goals, 69–70
    and knowing limits, 65–67
    poor decisions, 61–62, 64
    and risk-taking, 67–69
    and sense of self, 63
    and "shoulds," 62–63
    taking control, 70–74
Department of Labor, Internet
    site, 199
Directories, for job search
    information, 186, 187, 188, 189
Directory of Advertisers, 189
Directory of Executive Recruiters,
    188–189, 215
Directory of Insurance Companies, 189
Discussion lists, Internet, 196

Education, résumé, 96–97
Employment agencies, 211
    private agencies, 211
    temp agencies, 211
Encyclopedia of Associations, 187,
    189, 203
Enthusiasm
    and job interview, 138–139
    on Lifeline, 41
    and success, 37–39, 41–43
Events for career development,
    217–222
    career forums, 219–220
    conventions, 218–219
    guidelines for use, 220–222
    job fairs, 219
    mentoring programs, 218
    workshops, 219
Executive recruiters
    directory of, 188–189
    role of, 212–213

Federal Information Service,
    phone number for, 212

Federal Job Opportunities
     Electronic Bulletin Board, 194
Finding a Job on the Internet, 193
Focus, and interviews, 146–147
Fortune, 188
Future
  creating vision, 19
  on Lifeline, 16
  looking forward, 15–16

Gender issues
  for men, 4
  for women, 5
Glamorous opportunities,
     limitations of, 58–59
Goals
  and clarity, 23
  and decision-making, 69–70
  examples of, 17
  and vision, 19–20
Government agencies
  employment services, 211–212
  information service phone
     number, 212
  Internet job information, 194, 199
Guide to Executive Recruiters, 189,
     215
Guide to Internet Job Searching, 193

Hidden requirements of job,
     153–54
Human relations
  on Lifeline, 41
  and success, 39–40
  types of skills, 93

Identity
  and integrity, 173–177
  and values, 169–170

Informational/referral interviews,
     124–131, 146–147,
     149–151
  active participation in,
     126–127
  appearance for, 128
  approach to, 127
  end of interview, 128
  objectives of, 149–150
  positive aspects of, 124–125
  preparation for, 127–128,
     132
  protocol for, 127–129
  scheduling interviews,
     125–126
  strategic review of, 130–131
  tracking information from,
     128–129
Information about jobs
  career services, 209–216
  events for career development,
     217–222
  Internet, 191–200
  networking, 201–208
  printed material, 183–190
Infoseek, 192
*Insider's Guide to Small Business
     Resources*, 188
Integrity
  action steps for, 177–178
  and identity, 173–177
  on Lifeline, 177
  and professional identity,
     174–177
Internet, 191–200
  bookmarking sites, 194, 198
  compiling resource list from,
     194
  discussion lists, 196
  federal job listings, 194
  guidelines for job search,
     196–200
  job banks, 194–195
  job sites, 193–194
  on-line career centers, 194

Internet (*cont.*)
  organization of, 191–192
  résumé banks, 195
  search, refinement of,
    198–199
  search engines, 192, 197, 198,
    199, 200
  service providers, 192
  software/hardware requirements
    for, 191
  use at library, 192–193
  USENET newsgroups, 196
  Web addresses, 193–194
Internet Yellow Pages, The, 193
Interviews
  contact letters, 150–151,
    153–156
  for focused person, 146–147
  follow-up letters, 128,
    157–158
  and hidden requirements of job,
    153–154
  informational/referral
    interviews, 124–131,
    149–151
  job interview, 133–139
  pre-interview decisions about
    candidates, 152
  referral interviews, 148–149
  for unfocused person,
    146–147
  for very focused person,
    146–147

Job assessment centers, 210
Job banks, Internet, 194–195
Job fairs, 219
Job interview, 133–139, 146
  and appearance, 139
  and attitude, 138–139
  follow-up letter, 157–158
  initiating contact for, 153–154
  objectives of, 151–153

preparation for, 134–135
purpose of, 133–134
and résumé, 135–138
Jobs with capes, 58–59

Leadership, forms of, 92
Letters
  follow-up to interview, 128,
    157–158
  to keep in touch with job
    contacts, 158
  requesting job interview,
    150–151, 153–156
  tailoring to job listing,
    154–156
Library
  for accessing Internet,
    192–193
  for job search information,
    183–185
LifeCircle
  identifying network, 115–116,
    118–119
  for understanding personal
    balance, 75–78
  for values, 170
  volunteer activities, 166
Life events, significance for career,
    55–56
Lifeline
  future in, 16
  integrity on, 177
  personal history on, 33–36, 41
  purpose of, 14
  and risk-taking, 68
Life stage, and vision, 26–27
LISTSERVs, 196
Lycos, 192, 198

Magazines, for job search
  information, 185–186, 188

Management skills, forms of, 93

Mancuso's Small Business Resource Guide, 188

Mentoring
mentoring programs, 218
role of mentor, 218

Microsoft Explorer, 191, 195

Mindfulness, 19

Mullins, Patricia A., 229–230

Myers-Briggs Personality Type Indicator, 210

National Association of Personnel Consultants, 211

National Business Employment Weekly, 186

National Trade and Professional Associations of the United States, 186–187, 203

Netscape Navigator, 191, 195

Networking
action steps, 120
and clubs, 204
and community, 203–204
creating networks, 117
guidelines for, 203–210
identifying network, 115–116
for job-seekers, 201–208
joining network, 116–117
and LifeCircle, 115–116, 118–119
new approach to, 107–108
old approach to, 106–107
and professional associations, 203
at schools attended, 202
and shared activities, 118–119
strategic networking, 111–114, 117

Newspapers, for job search information, 185–186, 188

Objective statement, résumé, 91–92, 100, 136

Office of Personnel Management, Career America Connection, 212

Off to Work, 230

Opportunity tracking
action steps, 140–141
and informational/referral interviews, 124–131
and job interview, 133–139
and self-direction, 122–124
in work setting, 131–133, 159–162

Organization, time-management, 143–144

Outplacement services, 212

Past
finding patterns in, 36–37
personal history, 30–44
and self-understanding, 30–36
work history, 45–60

Personal history
action steps for construction of, 43–44
on Lifeline, 33–36, 41
patterns and past, 36–37
people skills in, 39–40
signs of enthusiasm in, 37–39, 41–43
understanding past, 30–36

Preferences
exercise for focus on, 53–54
work-related, examples of, 52–53

Present
finding opportunities in, 70–74
importance of, 24
vision for, 19

Printed materials, 183–190
bookstore, 185
directories, 186, 187, 188, 189

Printed materials (*cont.*)
  guidelines for use of, 186–190
  library for, 183–185
  magazines, 185–186, 188
  newspapers, 185–186, 188
  types of reference works, 186,
    187, 188, 189
Prodigy, 192
Professional associations
  and networking, 203
  publications of, 185, 186, 189
Proposals
  to improve present position,
    160–161
  for original projects, 162–164
  white paper proposal, 159–160

Qualifications, résumé, 92–94

Referral interviews, 148–149
  initiation of contact for,
    148–150
  objects of, 148
  See also Informational/referral
    interviews
Résumé, 81–105
  achievements, 84–91, 94–95,
    97–98
  action steps for, 103–105
  ah-ha resume examples, 89–90
  best achievements reflected in,
    84–91
  communication skills in, 92–93,
    94–95, 99
  computer scanning of, 135
  development, examples of,
    101–103
  education, 96–97
  gearing format toward position,
    136
  human relations skills in, 93

  information about self provided
    in, 92–94, 99
  and job interview, 135–138
  leadership skills in, 92
  management skills in, 93
  myths/tricks/fears related to,
    82–83
  objective statement, 91–92, 100,
    136
  ongoing improvement of,
    119–120, 140
  outcome focus in, 99
  as primary resource, 137–138
  purposes of, 83–84, 95, 99
  qualifications, 92–94
  special achievements/awards,
    97–98
  technical expertise in,
    93, 97
  work/related experience,
    95–96
Résumé banks, Internet, 195
Risk-taking, 67–69
  avoiding anxiety, 67–68
  and decision-making, 61–74
  and Lifeline, 68

Schools
  and networking, 202
  school career services, 210
Search engines, Internet, 192, 197,
  198, 199, 200
Self
  events shaping reality for, 14–15
  knowing limits for, 65–67
  relationship with work, 12–13
  self-recognition, importance of,
    30–31
  and understanding past, 30–36
Self-descriptions, types of, 12
Self-direction, and opportunity
  tracking, 122–124
Sense of humor, importance of, 18

Service providers, Internet, 192
"Shoulds," examples in career,
    62–63
Small Business Sourcebook, 187
State, employment services of,
    211–212
Strategy
    action steps, 165–166
    development of, 113–114
    examples of, 109–111
    focus on, 4
    meaning of, 2, 108
    strategic networking, 111–114,
        117
    strategic thinking, questions in,
        108
Strong Interest Inventory,
    210
Success
    and enthusiasm, 37–39
    and human relations, 39–40
    and true self, 40–43

Taking control
    action steps for, 78
    becoming director of career,
        123
    examples of, 71–74
    steps toward, 70–71
    supplicants versus applicants,
        122–123
Technical expertise, forms of,
    93
Temporary agencies, 211
Time-management, 143–144
    tools for, 143–144
Training, in résumé, 96–97

United Migrant Opportunity
    Services, 212
USENET newsgroups, 196

Values
    and identity, 169–170
    LifeCircle for, 170
    in workforce, 20
    and workplace, 170–173
Veterans' Affairs Regional Offices,
    212
Virtual workplace, 22
Vision
    action steps in formation of,
        27–28
    and changing workplace,
        21–22
    and clarity, 24–26
    and goals, 19–20
    and life stage, 26–27
    for past/present/future, 19
    uniqueness of, 26
Vocational tests, 210
Volunteering, 164–165
    benefits of, 164–165
    LifeCircle for, 166

Wall Street Journal, The, 188
White paper proposal,
    159–160
Work, self and relationship with,
    12–13
Work experience, résumé,
    95–96
Work history, 45–60
    achievements, 47–52
    action steps for understanding,
        60
    and career path, 57–58
    and future planning, 46–47
Work history (*cont.*)
    to shape present career,
        54–56
    skills/preferences, 52–54
Workplace
    changes related to, 21–22
    personality of, 171

and values, 170–173
virtual workplace, 22
Workplace opportunities, 131–133,
    159–162
improving present position,
    160–161
white paper proposal,
    159–160
Work proposal, 162–164
initiating opportunity for

submission, 163–164
objectives of, 162–163
purpose of, 162
Workshops, and job search,
    219
World Wide Web. *See* Internet

Yahoo!, 192, 197, 198, 199

Patricia V. Alea

Pat has a B.A. and an M.A. in English and began her career as a secondary teacher. Her interest quickly expanded into adult education, community, and human service settings, where she began helping others articulate and promote their visions. During the past twenty years Pat has developed a variety of "values-based" marketing systems to help individuals identify personal goals as a way to drive organizational success. As director of marketing for the Wisconsin Alumni Association, Pat initiated career-related seminars and services for students and alumni. She is a frequent keynote speaker and continues to consult nationally on a wide range of marketing topics. She teaches at the University of Wisconsin–Madison's Grainger School of Business in the Small Business Development Center.

Patricia A. Mullins

Patty has a Ph.D. in cognitive psychology from the University of Chicago and has been involved in teaching and research for the past twenty years. As a professor at the University of Wisconsin–Madison, she has developed courses in program evaluation, industrial relations, and the psychology of work, blending theory with experience. In her consulting work, Patty has specialized in career and life planning for women. She has developed a national mentoring program for University of Wisconsin alumnae and a model university-community partnership project to foster the success of single-parent students. Patty is often called upon as an expert witness on employment issues, and her research has been reported in the *Wall Street Journal*.

Together, Pat and Patty conduct seminars and workshops on career and life planning and consult with corporations to develop innovative workplace programs for performance enhancement. They host *Careertalk*, a regular hour-long broadcast on Wisconsin Public Radio, which combines work-related topics with advice to callers. They appear regularly on WISC-TV in a morning segment called *Off to Work*. They call their business Focus—on the Best Work of Your Life.

Co-authors Patricia A. Mullins (left) and
Patricia V. Alea. Photo by Larsen Photography

OTHER BOOKS OF INTEREST

The Way of the Leader by Donald G. Krause 0-399-52267-0/$12.00
For centuries, great leaders have followed the theories of Sun Tzu and
Confucius to win victories through effective use of leadership power. Now the
author reinterprets these leadership principles for the modern businessperson
working in today's volatile economic climate. *A Perigee Trade Paperback*

The Art of War for Executives by Donald G. Krause 0-399-51902-5/$12.00
Sun Tzu's 2,500-year-old Chinese text, *The Art of War*—with advice on
leadership, strategy, competition and cooperation—is adapted to modern
business practices. *A Perigee Trade Paperback*

The Adventure of Leadership
by Hap Klopp with Brian Tarcy 0-425-14376-7/$10.00
"Hap Klopp provides all the right reasons to break out of the corporate embalming
fluid and take on the adventure of leadership." —Harvey MacKay
A Berkley Trade Paperback

Deming Management Method *by Mary Walton* 0-399-55000-3/$13.95
W. Edwards Deming, the genius who revitalized Japanese industry, offers
his revolutionary system for overhauling American management.
A Perigee Trade Paperback

Deming Management at Work by Mary Walton 0-399-51685-9/$13.00
Practical applications of the highly acclaimed Deming Management Method.
A Perigee Trade Paperback

Not for Bread Alone by Konosuke Matsushita 0-425-14133-0/$12.00
From one of the century's most accomplished business leaders comes a unique
and profoundly thoughtful approach to financial and personal achievement.
A Berkley Trade Paperback

Executive EQ by Robert K. Cooper, Ph.D., and Ayman Sawaf
0-399-52404-5/$14.95
The emotional intelligence equivalent of IQ, can be applied to corporate life
to achieve greater financial success and personal energy in the marketplace.
A Perigee Trade Paperback

Maximum Leadership by Charles M. Farkas and Philippe De Backer
0-399-52385-5/$15.00
The authors traversed North America, Europe, and Asia to interview
the heads of over 160 major multinational corporations. What they
discovered may forever change the way we look at business and our
roles as executives. *A Perigee Trade Paperback*

TO ORDER CALL: 1-800-788-6262, ext. 1, Refer to Ad #585

The Berkley Publishing Group
A member of Penguin Putnam Inc.
200 Madison Avenue
New York, NY 10016

*Prices subject to change